D1569606

Lifeline
BIOGRAPHIES

THE *GLEE* CAST
Inspiring Gleek Mania

by Felicity Britton

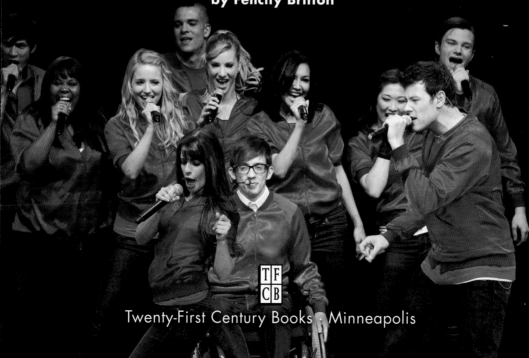

Twenty-First Century Books · Minneapolis

For Izzy and Luci

Twenty-First Century Books
A division of Lerner Publishing Group, Inc.
241 First Avenue North
Minneapolis, MN 55401 U.S.A.

Website address: www.lernerbooks.com

Library of Congress Cataloging-in-Publication Data

Britton, Felicity.
    The *Glee* Cast: Inspiring Gleek Mania / by Felicity Britton.
      p. cm. — (USA TODAY lifeline biographies)
    Includes bibliographical references and index.
    ISBN 978–0–7613–8639–1 (lib. bdg. : alk. paper)
    1. Glee (Television program)—Juvenile literature. 2. Television actors and actresses—United States—Biography—Juvenile literature. I. Title.
PN1992.77.G5558B75 2013
791.4502′80922—dc23 [B]   2011043706

Manufactured in the United States of America
1 – PP – 7/15/12

▶ **INTRODUCTION**
Glee!, 4

▶ **CHAPTER ONE**
Lea Michele and Chris Colfer, 10

▶ **CHAPTER TWO**
Dianna Agron
and Cory Monteith, 30

▶ **CHAPTER THREE**
Amber Riley and Mark Salling, 44

▶ **CHAPTER FOUR**
Jenna Ushkowitz
and Harry Shum Jr., 58

▶ **CHAPTER FIVE**
Kevin McHale, Heather Morris,
and Naya Rivera, 70

▶ **CHAPTER SIX**
Jane Lynch
and Matthew Morrison, 86

▶ Source Notes, 100
▶ Selected Bibliography, 105
▶ Further Reading and Websites, 108
▶ Index, 110

Season 1: The core cast of the first season of *Glee* poses for a photo. They are *(back row, left to right)* Chris Colfer, Jenna Ushkowitz, Matthew Morrison, Cory Monteith; *(middle row)* Kevin McHale, Lea Michele, Amber Riley; *(front)* Jessalyn Gilsig (who played the wife of teacher Will Schuester for the first two seasons of the show), Dianna Agron, Mark Salling, Jane Lynch, and Jayma Mays.

Glee!

It's spawned more *Billboard* Hot 100 singles than Elvis and the Beatles. It's won an Emmy, a SAG award, a Peabody, a GLAAD (Gay & Lesbian Alliance Against Defamation) award, the best television comedy series from the Golden Globe Awards, and a Worst TV Show of the Week condemnation from the Parents Television Council. The pilot (the first show of a potential series) in 2009 was watched by more than 10 million people.

"By its very definition, Glee is about opening yourself up to joy."

—*Glee* pilot, inscription in a trophy case, 2009

Set in a fictionalized version of Lima, Ohio, *Glee* is a television show about a group of outcasts. They include a super-talented nerd who dreams of success on Broadway, a boy in a wheelchair, a gay loner, an overweight diva, and a cheerleader and a jock who have to weigh their love of performing with their desire for popularity. Together they form a family of sorts in their high school glee club. Led by their Spanish teacher, Mr. Schuester, the club is constantly undermined by the school's ruthless cheerleading coach, Sue Sylvester, who makes it her mission to destroy the club.

Award winning: The cast and producers of *Glee,* along with cocreator Ryan Murphy *(center front holding statue)* celebrate their win at the Golden Globe awards for Best Television Series—Musical or Comedy in 2010.

April 9, 2009

Hit show 'Glee' sings to anyone who ever felt like an outsider

<u>From the Pages of</u>
<u>USA TODAY</u>

Glee follows a motley crew of outcasts, jocks and cheerleaders who are trying to restore a once-renowned glee club at William McKinley High School in Lima, Ohio. The students deal with a variety of topical issues: sex, relationships, competition, cliques. The adults have their issues, too.

It's about the music

For many viewers, *Glee* has made the uncool cool. Fans have downloaded more than 4.7 million of the songs performed by the cast in the show, according to Nielsen SoundScan. Two soundtracks have sold more than 1.3 million units. Producers added four shows to a cast concert tour to meet heavy demand.

The cast taped an *Oprah* episode dedicated to the show and were among performers at the White House Easter Egg Roll.

(Producer Ryan) Murphy says *Glee* has caught on because it's unique, not a cop or medical show, and has happy endings.

(Jane) Lynch (Sue Sylvester) says the pull is universal. "It's tapped into part of us that lives in the shadows, that we don't let people see, that's wanting to lift our voice in song and make a joyful noise," she says. That said, "People who dare to be who they are will get a slushie in the face."

Lynch says she has been approached by a broad range of fans, from children at the Kids' Choice Awards to a businessman in New York.

"He said, 'You know why I love that show? It's because it's about these kids standing in their own power and, in spite of everything else, saying I'm going to sing a song,'" she says.

'The show's about underdogs'

Despite the emphasis on music and comedy, *Glee* has its drama, too. Episodes have dealt with divorce, teen pregnancy and a boy coming out to his father.

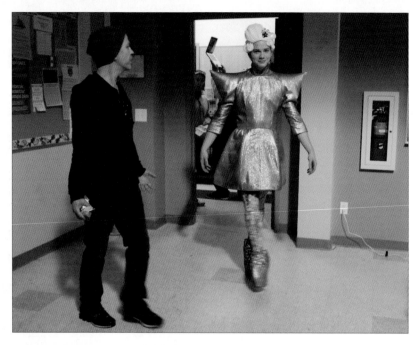

Walk this way: Chris Colfer *(right)* rehearses his walk as Kurt in a Lady Gaga costume for director Ryan Murphy in 2010. Murphy is also the series' cocreator and executive producer.

New episodes will touch on the treatment of women and teens' relationships with their parents. "I wanted very early, not only happy endings but to inform people. The show's about underdogs," Murphy says. "I wanted to talk about the underdog element in society: the pregnant girl, the gay kid, the kid in a wheelchair, the African-American girl who's one of five black kids in their school. I wanted to give voices to people who don't have voices."

Glee's Peabody award, which recognizes achievement and public service in the electronic media, cited "Wheels," an episode that focused on Artie (Kevin McHale), the singer who uses a wheelchair.

A small triumph for the downtrodden can be seen on set during a scene in which Kurt (Chris Colfer), clad in an outlandish silver costume, powdered wig and skyscraper heels, stands up to two jocks who push him and bubble-dressed Tina (Jenna Ushkowitz) into a locker to protest their [Lady] Gaga get-ups.

"It's showing off who you are," Kurt says, likening the outfits to football players wearing their uniforms to class. He has a voice, and it isn't just for singing.

—Bill Keveney

Glee combines comedy, drama, and music from a wide variety of genres. It also features characters to which many people can relate—characters who struggle with issues such as body image, sexuality, and especially self-acceptance. Instead of creating one-dimensional stereotypes, the writers have developed teenagers with strength, vulnerability, grace, awkwardness, anger, humor, hope, and talent—traits much like those of the real-life actors who play them.

Persistence Pays Off

Some of the Glee actors have been singing and dancing since they were toddlers. Others didn't start performing until high school or later. But none of them was handed opportunity on a silver platter. They created their own opportunities through hard work, dedication, and consistently showing up and trying again.

A typical week for the *Glee* cast begins with a six o'clock Monday morning call on the Paramount lot in Los Angeles, California. The average workday lasts twelve to fourteen hours. When not in a scene,

Behind the scenes: Lea Michele has her hair and makeup fixed between scenes on the set of *Glee* in 2009.

On tour: Members of the *Glee* cast perform in London, England, during the show's tour in 2011. The cast toured after both the 2010 and 2011 seasons.

the actors are rehearsing dance numbers or laying down vocal tracks in a recording studio. Each episode takes about eight days to complete. Weekends are reserved for press interviews and photo shoots. During breaks between seasons, the actors have performed in a live stage show and have shot a 3-D movie. They might just be the hardest-working cast in Hollywood!

Experiencing long hours and sudden fame has created a special bond for the young actors. This is obvious in the chemistry they share on-screen. While they may have come from very different backgrounds and taken very different routes to success, they all have one thing in common. They never stopped believing that if they worked hard enough and tried long enough, their dreams might just come true.

www.usatoday.com

USA TODAY
A GANNETT COMPANY

CHAPTER ONE

Supporting each other: *Glee* cast mates Chris Colfer and Lea Michele play friends and rivals Kurt and Rachel on the show. Here Chris attends the premiere of Lea's movie *New Year's Eve* (2011).

Lea Michele and Chris Colfer

■■■■■

Fiercely talented. Driven. Determined. Focused. These words not only sum up the character of Rachel Berry but the actress who plays her—Lea Michele. Lea describes Rachel as someone who acts in her everyday life as if she's performing for a huge audience. In one episode, Rachel says "I'm like Tinkerbell—I need applause to live." That line resonated with Lea, who practically grew up onstage (her first Broadway performance was as a child). The minute she read the first *Glee* script, she knew she wanted to play Rachel. She felt as if she understood her, as if Rachel was a part of her.

Lea Michele Sarfati was born in the Bronx, New York, on August 29, 1986. Her mom, Edith, is a Roman Catholic Italian American, and her dad, Marc, is a

Broadway baby: Lea (shown here as a toddler) grew up in New York and New Jersey. She started attending Broadway shows and got her first Broadway role in 1995 at the age of eight.

Spanish Sephardic Jew. Lea grew up learning about both religions. Marc ran a Jewish deli, and Edith was a registered nurse. Lea is their only child. When it was time to choose a school for Lea, her parents decided that she should go to school in nearby New Jersey. The family moved to Tenafly, New Jersey, where Lea attended elementary school.

When she was eight, Lea had a friend named Angela Hind whose family took Lea to see Broadway shows such as *Camelot*, *Cats*, and *Phantom of the Opera*. Lea fell asleep in *Camelot* and was scared at *Cats*. But *Phantom* ignited something in her. She loved the music and theatricality of the show and convinced her parents to buy her the sound track. For the next few days, she played it constantly, memorizing the song "Angel of Music."

Just a few days after attending *Phantom*, Angela was due to attend an open call for the part of Young Cosette in the show *Les Misérables* (or, *Les Miz*). Angela's dad became ill and ended up in the hospital, so Lea's mom agreed to take Angela to the audition. Lea says, "I just thought it was fun 'cause my friend was doing it, so I was like, 'Eh! I'll do it, too!' And I was a really outgoing, funny kid, so I was just like 'Yeah! What the heck?'"

Broadway and Beyond

At the audition, Lea sang "Angel of Music" and won the part. Her Broadway career had started. At eight, Lea played the role of Young Cosette in 1995 and 1996. Looking back, Lea says that the role of Young Cosette was the perfect place to start her acting career. "The great thing about starting off in *Les Miz* is that being a Young Cosette is really a great way of stepping in to the business because you learn so much so quickly. The size of the role, the amount of work that they put on me was just enough. I also was lucky to have people like our stage manager and [executive producer] Richard Jay-Alexander and my conductor and fellow cast members of *Les Miz* so it was like a lesson right there that got me to understand what I was doing since I basically came into this with nothing, knowing actually nothing about theatre or acting or anything. Neither did my family—we didn't know anything!"

After a year and a half, Lea had grown too old for the part of Young Cosette. But just a few weeks after leaving *Les Miz*, she auditioned for a show called *Ragtime* that was being staged in Toronto, Ontario. Before she knew it, she and her mother were packing their bags and relocating to Canada. Between performances Lea's mom homeschooled her. Lea was away from her dad and the family dog and two cats for an entire year. But her family believed that the acting and singing experience would be an opportunity not to be missed. Lea credits her parents' easygoing nature and that she was an only child as factors in her success. Because she had no other children, Lea's mom was able to

Role in *Ragtime*: Lea *(front left)* and other cast members of *Ragtime* perform at the 1998 Tony Awards. The Tony Awards recognize excellence in live Broadway theater.

give up her nursing job to help Lea full-time and to shuttle her to and from shows. Lea saw many other parents really pushing their children and saying, "You have to get this job." Her parents typically said things like "It's no big deal."

In 1998 Lea's efforts were rewarded when she won the role of the Little Girl (Tateh's daughter) for the original Broadway cast of *Ragtime*. When she went to high school, Lea took some time away from Broadway. In her senior year, she played Shprintze and Chava in the Broadway revival of the musical *Fiddler on the Roof*. When not acting, she worked in a dress shop, cleaning and vacuuming.

During Lea's Broadway gigs, her parents rented an apartment in Manhattan (New York). Lea split her time among her family, friends, and school in Tenafly and her mainly adult costars onstage in New York. Lea admits she had to grow up pretty fast. You can't exactly throw tantrums and act immature around Broadway legends such as Marin Mazzie, Audra McDonald, and Brian Stokes Mitchell (who went on to play one of Rachel's dads on *Glee*). But Lea says she wouldn't change any of it. It was exactly where she wanted to be.

Being Different

Although accepted on Broadway, Lea was experiencing rejection elsewhere. She looked different from the girls at her high school, where being popular meant being thin and blonde. Lea remembers watching TV shows such as *Gossip Girl* and *90210* and being aware of how beautiful and admired the characters were. "When I was in high school, when I was 16, I would watch shows growing up and say 'Oh, she's so beautiful, . . . or she's so cool. I wish I could be as cool as she is. I wish I could be as popular.' I never watched a show and said, 'Oh my God, I looked like that. I did that. I understand that. I felt like that.' That's what's so great about *Glee*; teens can absolutely identify with it. There's people to look up to and people to identify with. It's what real high school students are like."

Teachers were not sympathetic that Lea was tired from her late nights on the stage. In fact, they seemed to go out of their way not to cast her in school plays or allow her to sing solos in choir. Lea was on the debate team and played volleyball but definitely felt like a loser among the cool kids. Auditioning for TV parts was tough too. Managers and casting directors told her she looked too ethnic, her nose was too big, and she looked too Jewish. Several people suggested she should get a nose job and that she just wasn't pretty enough for TV. Lea hoped that one day, somehow, she would find people just like her who would accept her for who she was.

While still in high school, Lea started workshops for a new rock musical called *Spring Awakening*. During this time, Lea had to decide whether to attend college or pursue acting full-time. She had been accepted into New York University's Tisch School of the Arts CAP21 program. But she decided that she wanted to stay with *Spring Awakening*, figuring she could always go back to college later.

BFF

After several years of development, *Spring Awakening* premiered Off-Broadway, running from May through August 2006. It opened on

Workshops are staged readings of a new play that is still being developed. Following the readings, the director, the cast, and the crew talk about how to change the play to make improvements. If the play is a musical, the team might decide to add or remove a song to help improve the story.

Broadway on December 10, 2006. Lea was twenty and played the role of Wendla, a main character. Jonathan Groff (who plays Jesse St. James on *Glee*) played Lea's love interest, Melchior, and the two instantly became best friends. *Spring Awakening* was a huge hit and was nominated for eleven Tony Awards—the Broadway equivalent of the Academy Awards (or Oscars). Many celebrities and theater folk went to see *Spring Awakening*. But the most important audience member for Lea was Ryan Murphy. Ryan saw the show and later

Best friends: Jonathan Groff and Lea pose in their costumes for *Spring Awakening* in 2007. The two were on Broadway together and worked together again when Jonathan guest starred on *Glee* starting in 2009.

met Lea at a dinner she attended with Jonathan. Ryan had cast Jonathan in a TV pilot called *Pretty/Handsome*. At the dinner, Ryan told Lea that if *Pretty/Handsome* wasn't picked up by a TV network, he was thinking about doing another show called *Glee*. There was a role in that show that would be perfect for her.

Hello, Hollywood

Jonathan and Lea both left *Spring Awakening* at the same time. After some solo shows at a cabaret club in New York, Lea headed to California to sing the part of Eponine in the *Les Misérables in Concert* series. She thought that as long as she was in Los Angeles for a few months, she would try out for a few TV shows. In the first audition for *Glee*, she sang the song "On My Own" from *Les Miz*. The piano player skipped a verse. Instead of going with it, Lea stopped singing and went over and told the player to go back and start again from the second verse. The producers and casting director burst out laughing. They laughed again during her reading, and Lea rebuked them. "That wasn't supposed to be funny! That was my serious part. Now I'm going to do it again and I want you all to cry." She didn't realize it at the time, but she was acting just as they had imagined Rachel Berry would act.

On her way to her second *Glee* audition, Lea got into a serious car accident. But she was determined not to miss the interview. She left her

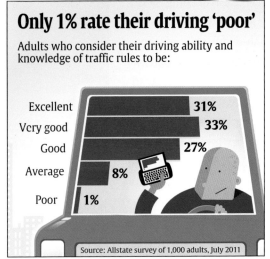

USA TODAY Snapshots®

Only 1% rate their driving 'poor'

Adults who consider their driving ability and knowledge of traffic rules to be:

Excellent	31%
Very good	33%
Good	27%
Average	8%
Poor	1%

Source: Allstate survey of 1,000 adults, July 2011

By Anne R. Carey and Paul Trap, USA TODAY, 2011

Family support: Lea had the support of her parents, Marc Sarfati and Edith Sarfati, as she worked to achieve her singing and acting dreams in high school. They are shown here in 2009.

totaled car on the street and ran to the studio, picking pieces of glass out of her hair in front of the amazed executives. Once again, this determination and focus reflected exactly what they had in mind for the character of Rachel. Lea says, "Rachel is very determined and I was that girl in high school. I was the one who knew what she wanted and who she was and wasn't going to get side-tracked by the more silly stuff that people get obsessed with in high school like partying. I was not like that at all. I was way more like Rachel."

Family Ties

Lea got the part on *Glee*. She was ecstatic. For most of the cast, this was their big TV break and they were all becoming famous together. The long hours in rehearsal and shooting and dealing with all the media attention were a bonding experience. Lea had finally found people just like her who accepted her for who she was—just like Rachel Berry had

First Wives Club: Lea *(second from right)* has become friends with many of her cast mates. She is especially close to *(left to right)* Dianna Agron, Jenna Ushkowitz (whom she has known since they were children), and Amber Riley.

found in glee club. Even though they spend so much time together on set, Lea and her cast mates get together after work, often hanging out and cooking. Lea shared a house for six months with Dianna Agron before getting her own apartment. She sees Dianna, Jenna, and Amber almost every day. The cast even has a nickname for the actresses—First Wives Club.

Lea's bonded with others over tattoos (she has fourteen so far). She's convinced Jenna and Kevin that all three of them should get matching "Imagine" tattoos on their left feet. So far Lea's tattoos include a little gold star for her character Rachel, a blue butterfly on her back that she and her mom got together, another butterfly on her foot, the song title "I Believe" from *Spring Awakening* on her wrist, two musical notes from the song "Bohemian Rhapsody" by the rock band Queen on her left shoulder, a bird on her hip, and a tattoo on her thigh in memory of her late grandfather. She says she may get more tattoos to commemorate other significant events in her life. But so far, she doesn't have a tattoo for being included in the 2010 *Time* 100. This *Time* magazine list of the most influential people in the world cited her as an inspiration for musical programs in schools.

Future Plans

Lea finds time in her busy schedule to do many things. For example, in 2011 she filmed *New Year's Eve* with Ashton Kutcher, Zac Efron, and Sarah Jessica Parker. Lea will also play the part of Dorothy in the animated movie *Dorothy of Oz*. She says her nature is to just not stop. People around her have to tell her to slow down. She has dreams of playing more roles in Broadway shows and wants to act in more movies.

She does find some time to relax through cooking, baking, collecting records, and hiking. Most nights you'll find her at home watching reality TV, taking a bath, or Skyping friends in New York. She's not very interested in the Hollywood party and club scene. She says taking drugs or drinking would be impossible with her schedule, and she's too determined to succeed in her career to risk going down that path.

When *Seventeen* magazine asked Lea what she would tell her seventeen-year-old self or other teens, she replied, "I would tell 17-year-olds to be proud of who you are. Don't try to change yourself for others. Focus on school and your future. Boys and friends will come and go, just focus on you and your future."

Movie star: Lea made her movie debut in *New Year's Eve* in 2011. She costarred in the movie with Ashton Kutcher *(left)*.

May 10, 2010

Lea Michele never stopped believing

From the Pages of
USA TODAY

Lea Michele won't let you rain on her parade.

Michele, one of the breakout stars of Fox's musical comedy *Glee*, is a tiny, petite wisp who speaks in soft, dulcet [pleasing] tones. But in person, she's formidable.

"I always knew what I wanted to do," says Michele, 23. And that was being on stage.

The series showcases Michele's acting, dancing and singing talents, has garnered her a Golden Globe nomination and launched her as TV's newest triple threat. Has it sunk in yet that she's on the hottest show on TV, or on the list of *Time* magazine's 100 most influential people in the world for, as assistant managing editor Radhika Jones says, being "such a talented person with so much room to grow and explore"? Well, yes and no, Michele says.

"We've been doing this for a really long time and we're constantly in work mode. Every now and then, I have blissful moments of thanking God for all the amazing things that are happening," she says. "When I leave the White House after just meeting [President] Obama or when I see my face on the cover of *Rolling Stone* or when I meet someone who tells me that their daughter is inspired by me, those are moments that are incredibly joyful."

Embracing the weirdo

"Rachel is very much like me when I was about 10 to 12, working in theater, very driven. When I was in high school, although I wasn't like Rachel, I understand her. I was similar in the sense that I didn't conform to what people thought was cool. It was important to do what I believed in," Michele says.

Chris Colfer—from Outcast to Icon

Imagine going from working in a dry-cleaning shop to winning a Golden Globe and being included in *Time* magazine's 100 Most Influential People

That focus on her goal enabled her to have self-assurance at an age when most of her peers were grappling with insecurity and a need to conform.

"I knew what I wanted to do and what I wanted to be, and I kept that in my head at all times. I'd been working since I was 8. I saw the real world when I was 8, and I knew (my school) Tenafly High School was not the real world. It was OK to be different shapes, sizes, whatever," Michele says.

Being on the show, Michele says, "has taught me that about myself. It really praises your differences, and it's helped me embrace mine." In person, Michele exudes confidence in herself and her attributes. And

Eye on the prize: Lea sees a lot of herself in the character she plays on *Glee*. She admits she has always been very focused on achieving her show biz dreams.

"she has a lot of belief in her talent," [*Glee* cocreator Ryan] Murphy says.

But when she was first in Hollywood and trying to break into TV, Murphy says, "she was worried if she would find her way. She's not blond and anorexic. I love that she's gone from Rachel Berry to a red carpet darling and arguably the young actress that every designer is dying to dress. Her beauty is her own, just like Barbra Streisand's beauty was her own."

Murphy has no doubt that Michele will achieve her goals. "She's very ambitious and driven, and she's got her eye on the prize. She's always been focused," he says. "Talking to her mother, she's been that way from birth."

—Donna Freydkin

list in just two years. That's what happened to Chris Colfer, who plays *Glee*'s Kurt Hummel. His portrayal of the bullied, gay high school student has given many real-life teens a role model they hadn't seen on TV before.

"The show has struck a chord with an audience that never had anything to relate to before. I know personally, because I am that audience, I'm one of those kids," Chris says. "It's the first time that the performing arts have been put in a good light and been encouraged. And yes, there are still virgins in this world, and our show is full of them."

Chris identifies with the underdogs and outcasts of the show. He says his high school experience was absolutely horrible. He was at the bottom of the high

Award winner: Chris Colfer holds his Golden Globe statue for Best Supporting Actor in 2011. In his speech, he reached out to kids who are bullied at school.

school food chain. So he definitely relates to kids who are teased for being who they are. Accepting his Golden Globe in 2011, Chris added a serious note. "To all the amazing kids that watch our show and the kids that our show celebrates, who are constantly told 'no' by the people in their environments, by bullies at school that they can't be who they are or have what they want because of who they are. Well, screw that, kids."

Fashion, High or Low?

Chris can relate to many aspects of Kurt's personality, but the character's obsession with fashion is not one of them. Despite Kurt's love for

Fashion hound: Chris wore this outfit in the second-season finale of *Glee* in 2011. The character of Kurt loves fashion and wears eye-catching ensembles. Chris says he is the opposite of the character when it comes to what he likes to wear in real life.

design houses such as Burberry, Marc Jacobs, and Alexander McQueen, Chris is definitely not someone who spends a lot of money on clothes.

"I get all my clothes from Target. That's my favorite store. The ladies who dress us on the show always make fun of me for it," he says. He says he sees outfits in magazines, TV, or fashion shows and thinks, 'There's no WAY anyone would wear anything like that' only to find a similar outfit at his next costume fitting. He often thinks his costumes are pranks. But they're not.

Finding His Passion

Chris was born on May 27, 1990, and grew up in Clovis, California. Chris was interested in film and TV from an early age. He loved movies, TV, and escapism. He always wanted to be on the other side of the screen, participating—not watching.

November 11, 2009

Baby-faced Chris Colfer leaps into 'Glee,' his acting target

From the Pages of
USA TODAY

Chris Colfer can relate to many of the quirks of his *Glee* character, Kurt Hummel.

Like Kurt, Colfer was an outsider in high school, hanging out mostly with the lunch ladies. He was involved in the writing club and theater. And, like Kurt, "I'm very competitive, but I don't think I'm superior to anyone. I'm just this wimp."

Actually, he's a nice guy, says Colfer's co-star Cory Monteith, who plays quarterback and high school hunk Finn.

"Chris is one of those very rarely occurring actors. You don't see people that are that original and talented and humble and nice all rolled into one," Monteith says.

While taking freshman classes at Fresno City College, he met with *Nip/Tuck*'s Ryan Murphy about a new musical show he was developing.

Murphy was so impressed with Colfer that he wrote the role of Kurt for him, which still shocks the newbie actor.

—Donna Freydkin

Chris's sister, Hannah, was born with severe epilepsy. Her body has about fifty seizures an hour, every hour of the day. She has been in and out of hospitals her whole life. "Chris was absolutely selfless when it came to his sister—he gave up a great deal of his social life for her," says his mom. "People would ask 'Are you going to become a doctor so you can find a cure for your sister?' And he would say, 'I'm going to grow up and become a famous actor so I can pay someone ELSE tons of money to find a cure.'"

Family support: Chris's parents were very supportive of his desire to be a performer. Here Chris and his parents are shown with his younger sister, Hannah, in the 1990s.

Chris's mom, Karyn, remembers watching Chris in his first role at the age of eight, playing Snoopy. She says she saw something ignite in Chris that never turned off. Her sensitive child—prematurely mature because of his sister's condition and gifted academically—had found his outlet. Chris's mom and dad committed to ensuring Chris could pursue performing.

Getting His Start

Chris started performing with Oral Interp, a local group that presented written stories. That led to school plays and then to community theater. Between the ages of nine and fourteen, Chris performed in community theater plays such as *A Christmas Carol*, *The Sound of Music*, and *Oliver!* four nights a week. He took a few singing and tap dancing lessons and, at fourteen, acted as assistant director for a play, *America!* It benefited the Valley Children's Hospital.

At Clovis East High School (CEHS), Chris was involved in drama, edited his school's literary magazine, and was active in speech and debate. He placed ninth in the state competition for dramatic interpretation. He also worked mornings in the school's cafeteria. He says that the women who worked in the cafeteria were some of his closest friends from high school. He still stays in touch with them. While other kids socialized after school, Chris was rehearsing or performing in plays, caring for his sister, or staying home writing.

Chris says he was a total Rachel Berry in high school—an

overachieving, underappreciated kid. He was involved in lots of activities, but they didn't bring any social success. For example, he was president of the writer's club. But he was also the only member of the writer's club. He says that pretty much sums up his high school experience.

Chris was overweight, with braces, freckles, and his distinctive high-pitched voice. He says that at one point, he lost 40 pounds (18 kilograms), thinking it would make him more popular. But nothing changed. All it did was make him feel like a skinny loser instead of a fat loser.

These days, the kids who once teased him in the hallways by calling him "fag" or "freak" are contacting him on his Facebook page with claims of what good times they had together. Chris's success has been a satisfying form of redemption. He offers advice to kids dealing with bullies: "When people hurt you over and over, think of them like sand paper. They may scratch and hurt you a bit but in the end, you end up polished and they end up useless."

Chris's high school experience is echoed on *Glee*. On the show, Chris's character is bullied by the other students, particularly jock Dave Karofsky, played by Max Adler. Later episodes revealed that Karofsky was torturing Kurt because he was struggling with his own feelings of being attracted to men.

High Anxiety

In his senior year, Chris got the lead role in a comedic short film called *Russel Fish: The Sausage and Eggs Incident*. The film was shot in June 2008 in Fresno, California. While the film was well received at film festivals, Chris's career was not looking as promising. He enrolled in Fresno City College, a community college with a performing arts division. A family friend was acting as his agent and sent him on numerous auditions with no luck. Chris says he's horrible at auditions, calling them his weakness.

He was ready to give up on acting when he received news of the *Glee* audition. Chris was an enormous fan of producer Ryan Murphy's FX series *Nip/Tuck*. The idea of auditioning in front of his idol petrified

October 19, 2010

Gay teens told 'It Gets Better'

From the Pages of USA TODAY

They sit down in front of the camera, and they start to talk. In English, in Spanish, in American Sign Language. Proudly wearing their U.S. Marine uniforms or wedding rings or holding squiggly, giggling children. Most of them gay, each has a message for gay teenagers who may be contemplating suicide. "It gets better!" these adults tell them, in heartfelt videos posted to a new YouTube channel.

A string of suicides by gay youth nationwide this fall impelled many of them to tell their stories online, speaking of the harassment and bullying they endured in middle and high school.

Studies have shown that gay teens are four times more likely to attempt suicide than straight teens. There's no evidence to suggest that being gay intrinsically [automatically] makes teens more suicide-prone. Instead, "the high level of stigma from society and external pressures significantly increase the risk for suicide for these kids," says Caitlin Ryan, a researcher at San Francisco State University.

Teens "often feel like they're the only person who's going through what they're going through, and these videos will, we hope, let them know that there are others who have gone through the same thing and there is hope and there is help," says Charles Robbins, director of the Trevor Project, a suicide-prevention organization for gay, lesbian, bisexual and transgender youth that operates a 24/7 crisis hotline.

—Elizabeth Weise

him. In his nervousness, he dropped his script pages at the audition, scattering them all over the floor.

"Why do I have the feeling you've been Rolfe [the messenger boy] in *The Sound of Music* before?" asked Murphy.

"I was actually Kurt [one of the film's young Von Trapp children]." Chris answered. "I know, I have Von Trapp written all over me."

Chris was auditioning for the part of Artie, the *Glee* club member in a wheelchair. Afterward, he couldn't remember anything from the audition, other than that he had somehow managed to sing "Mr. Cellophane" from the musical *Chicago*. He was so nervous he felt as if he was going to get diarrhea.

A Role Just for Chris

Murphy hadn't seen anyone who looked or sounded like Chris before and was impressed with his talent. But he didn't give him the part. At least, not that part. Instead, Murphy got to work creating a new character especially for Chris, based largely on Murphy's own life. As a five-year-old, Murphy had confounded his parents by asking for a subscription to *Vogue* magazine. By seven he was ironing his own clothes and constantly performing in his bedroom with a hairbrush microphone in front of a mirror. His semipro hockey player dad was a little baffled but accepting, even when at the age of fifteen, Murphy told his father that he was gay. Murphy took his singing, love of fashion, and his relationship with his father and rolled it into the new character. He named the character Kurt Hummel after Chris's part in *The Sound of Music* and because Chris's rosy red cheeks reminded Murphy of the Hummel figurines his mother collected.

Joining the cast was a dream come true. Chris sings and dances and works with talented actors who have become his closest friends. Answering fan questions on chris-colfer.com, Chris said, "We're a big family behind the scenes. They're the best friends I've ever had, besides the CEHS kitchen staff. I'm close with everyone on a different level. Jenna and Amber are like my big sisters, Ryan Murphy and Dante Di Loreto [executive producer] are like Dads, and Jane Lynch is like the cool aunt you want to live with."

In 2011, at the age of twenty, Chris became the youngest-ever winner of the Golden Globe category Best Performance by an Actor in a Supporting Role in a Series, Mini-Series or Motion Picture Made for Television for his role as Kurt Hummel in *Glee*. He was also nominated for Outstanding Performance by a Male Actor in a Comedy Series at the 2011 Screen Actors Guild Awards. But perhaps the greatest accolade was his inclusion in *Time* magazine's 100 Most Influential People list. This mention praised the honesty in his acting and his role in empowering bullied youth.

Perfect pair: Darren Criss *(right)* is shown with Chris in 2011. Darren plays Blaine Anderson, Kurt's boyfriend, on *Glee*. He joined the show in the second season and has become a fan favorite.

Kurt's story line with Blaine Anderson, played by Darren Criss, has also been an inspiration for teens. The writers were committed to making the homosexual relationship as real and complex as the heterosexual romances. They hope that Kurt and Blaine's romance will continue to deliver a positive message to *Glee*'s audience. "I think what it says to a lot of young gay people who are confused and ashamed is that you can get love and are worthy of love."

Future Plans

In 2011 Chris's movie *Struck by Lightning* was sold and went into production. In addition to writing the screenplay, Chris stars alongside Dermot Mulroney, Christina Hendricks, and Allison Janney. Writing will likely be a part of Chris's future. He also sold the rights to a script for the pilot episode of *The Little Leftover Witch* (based on the children's book of the same name) to the Disney Channel and authored a book called *The Land of Stories*. He also sees himself on Broadway someday. And with his multiple skills, he might just achieve his dream of being the next Ryan Murphy and one day creating a TV show as phenomenal as *Glee*. Stay tuned!

The cheerleader and the jock: Dianna Agron and Cory Monteith play Quinn and Finn on *Glee*. Their characters were in a romantic relationship off and on in seasons 1 and 2.

Dianna Agron and Cory Monteith

In early 2009, Dianna Agron found herself in a Starbucks bathroom, urgently straightening her wavy, blonde hair. People were banging on the door, wanting to get in, and wondering what was taking her so long. "I'm so sorry," she called out. "I have a really important audition!"

Dianna was auditioning for the role of Quinn Fabray on a series to be called *Glee*. Instead of using the traditional casting calls, creator Ryan Murphy sought actors who could identify with the thrill of starring in theatrical roles. He spent three months attending Broadway shows, looking for talented but unknown actors. With only days until the pilot began filming, all the lead roles were filled except Quinn's.

At her audition, Dianna sang the classic song "Fly Me to the Moon," popularized by greats such as Johnny Mathis, Frank Sinatra, and many others. The producers were impressed but worried that Dianna might look too innocent to play the scheming ex-cheerleader Quinn. So they asked her to straighten her hair and come back wearing something less wholesome. Without time to go home, she raced to a nearby drugstore to buy a straightener. She did her hair in the bathroom at Starbucks and rushed back to the audition. By the end of the week, she'd been hired and started work. She had no idea that by the end of the year, she would be nominated for the Teen Choice Award for Breakout Female Star and a Screen Actors Guild Award.

All smiles: Dianna showed an interest in dancing and performing from a very young age.

A Born Performer

On April 30, 1986, Ronald and Mary Agron of Savannah, Georgia, welcomed their beautiful fair-haired baby, Dianna Charlotte. Ronald often called his baby Di or Charlie. Mary had her own special nickname for her—my lamb.

Later as an adult, Dianna would get a tattoo on her left rib cage that says "Mary had a little lamb" in reference to her mother.

Soon after Dianna was born, the Agron family moved to San Francisco, California, for her father's job as a general manager for Hyatt Hotels. Dianna's brother, Jason, was born in 1988. Dianna started dance classes at the age of three and loved performing. She says she was terribly clumsy, falling and tripping all the time. It was only when she danced that she was graceful. She also remembers that she loved playing circus in the backyard with Jason. Her favorite role was trapeze artist, aided by the swing set in her backyard. For a while, she thought she might have a future on the high wire.

Dianna loved to read, write, and draw for hours. She'd make believe she was characters from the books she loved, such as *Alice in Wonderland* and Roald Dahl's books. She was obsessed with actors Lucille Ball and Audrey Hepburn. She hoped to be a combination of both when she grew up. She was also crazy about animals. At one point, her family had two dogs, three rabbits, and four mice. She even groomed horses in the stable down the street in exchange for riding lessons.

A Spiritual Side

Dianna's father's family is originally from Russia. They immigrated to the United States in the early 1900s. An official at the immigration station at Ellis Island in New York determined their last name. The official felt that the name Agronsky was too Russian and altered it to Agron. Ron was raised

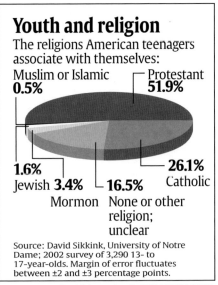

Youth and religion
The religions American teenagers associate with themselves:

Muslim or Islamic **0.5%** ⌐ Protestant **51.9%**

1.6% — **26.1%** Catholic
Jewish **3.4%** └ **16.5%**
Mormon   None or other religion; unclear

Source: David Sikkink, University of Notre Dame; 2002 survey of 3,290 13- to 17-year-olds. Margin of error fluctuates between ±2 and ±3 percentage points.

By Adrienne Lewis, USA TODAY, 2007

Bat Mitzvah

Bat Mitzvah literally means "daughter of commandment." According to Jewish law, when Jewish children reach thirteen years of age, they become responsible for their actions. Prior to a child reaching Bar or Bat Mitzvah, the child's parents hold the responsibility for the child following Jewish law and tradition. After this age, children bear their own responsibility for Jewish ritual law, tradition, and ethics and are able to participate in all areas of Jewish community life. The term also refers to the ceremony celebrating the milestone.

in the Jewish faith. When Dianna's mother decided to marry him, she converted to Judaism. The family attended temple, and at thirteen, Dianna had her Bat Mitzvah.

Dianna described her connection to the spiritual and traditional aspects of her faith. "I went to Sunday school, Hebrew school and a Jewish [day school] through third grade," she told the Jewish teen magazine *Jvibe*. "My brother and I loved everything about Hanukkah and Passover [Jewish holidays] and all the food." She added that she'd like to visit Israel and looks forward to celebrating other traditional milestones. "We're so scattered, so bar mitzvahs and weddings are the times we come together," she explains.

A Dance Background

During her elementary school years, Dianna continued to attend jazz and ballet classes. In fifth grade, she played Dorothy in a local production of *The Wizard of Oz*. As a teen, Dianna attended Burlingame High School near San Francisco and worked hard at her studies. She belonged to several clubs, including the musical theater club. She also led the yearbook team but claims she wasn't the most popular

Pretty as a picture: Dianna, shown here in her senior high school portrait, performed in plays in high school. She also took and taught dance classes.

girl in school. She says, "I definitely wasn't cool in high school. I really wasn't. I did belong to many of the clubs and was in leadership on yearbook and did the musical theater route, so I had friends in all areas. But I certainly did not know what to wear, did not know how to do my hair, all those things."

In her senior year of high school, she had roles in *Vanities* and *Grease*. And it was in high school that she began taking hip-hop dance classes and teaching dance to younger children. Competition for dance roles could be fierce, and the process prepared Dianna for the harsh world of Hollywood auditions.

"Having a dance background, I became used to rejection at an early age. Dance is very competitive, especially for a sensitive person like me. But I realized it's better not to take it so seriously. If you beat yourself up, it's hard to keep going."

Dianna is impressed that *Glee* recognizes that high school students have many aspects to their personalities. She says, "I think that [*Glee*] shows that regardless of who you are and what group you belong to, there are so many emotions behind each person in high school. Sometimes with teens, writers or directors short-change them and make them simple individuals, you're either the jock or the popular kid or the nerd. Everybody has those shades to them. This show, it really expands upon vulnerability and excitement and anger—all the experiences that you probably actually go through in high school."

Cheerio: Fans love (or love to hate) Dianna's *Glee* character, head cheerleader Quinn. But Quinn's layered story line encompasses a lot more than just being a cheerleader. Her character gave a baby up for adoption and dropped out of the glee club for a while.

Moving Toward Her Dream

Dianna graduated from high school with honors and decided to pursue acting as a career rather than go to college. With money from her Bat Mitzvah and from teaching dance, she moved to Los Angeles. She was soon getting small parts in TV shows such as *Shark*, *Drake* and *Josh*, and *CSI: NY*. This experience led to a recurring role in *Veronica Mars* and the role of Debbie Marshall in *Heroes*. She directed a music video for the band Thao with the Get Down Stay Down. She also wrote, directed, and acted in a short film called *A Fuchsia Elephant*.

In 2009 Dianna wrote a full-length screenplay, something that took a leap of confidence. She encourages her fans to break out of their comfort zones once a month, urging them to try something they don't think they'd be good at. She says the challenge is getting off the couch and putting your ideas into motion. There's always a reason not to try. But if you become fully invested, she says, you never know what could happen.

Playing Quinn Fabray on *Glee* has changed Dianna Agron's life in ways she could never have imagined. She's made new friends among the cast and the crew, been able to travel throughout the world, and has achieved her dream of making a living doing what she loves—performing. It's also led to film roles including small parts in the 2010 movies *Burlesque* and *The Romantics* and a leading role in the futuristic *I Am Number Four* (2011).

In her blog, she thanks *Glee* fans for their part in making her dream come true. She recognizes that her own dedication is paying off but also observes that without a committed fan base, she wouldn't have the luxury of going to work each day.

Fan friendly: Dianna signs autographs for fans outside the premiere of *Glee: The 3D Concert Movie* in Los Angeles, California, in August 2011.

Living in the Moment

Dianna's career options after *Glee* seem unlimited. She'd love to see her screenplay produced. More writing, movies, and directing seem certain. Meanwhile, though, she takes things one day at a time.

"My goal has always been not to look forward to the next thing, but to relish and celebrate the successes I have at the moment. Whether it's landing a part in a student film or having a good day in acting class, I never discredit anything. I believe in rewarding yourself too. With every job I've gotten, I've bought myself something. When *Glee* was picked up, I rented a piano for the year. For smaller victories, I'll go to dinner with a friend, or go for a walk and think about it all. It's important to say to yourself, 'Today was a good day.'"

Cory Monteith— Marching to the Beat of His Own Drum

On his Twitter account, 6 foot 3 (190-centimeter) Cory Monteith describes himself as a "tall, awkward, Canadian, actor, drummer, person."

This modest summary describes someone who is on a hit TV show, has a record deal with Columbia Records, and has met everyone

Tall talent: Cory Monteith *(left)* towers over some of his costars on *Glee*, such as Dianna. Finn and Quinn are friends on the show and in real life.

from President Obama to Oprah Winfrey to Sir Elton John. To say that playing Finn Hudson on *Glee* has changed Cory's life is an understatement too!

Born on May 11, 1982, in Calgary, Alberta, Cory Allan-Michael Monteith was raised in Victoria (the capital of the neighboring Canadian province of British Columbia). When his parents divorced, Cory, then seven years old, and his older brother, Shaun, were raised by his single mother, Ann McGregor. His dad, Joe, was a rifle sergeant in the Princess Patricia's Canadian Light Infantry, and the boys saw little of him. Unlike many of his *Glee* cast mates, Cory was not a singer, dancer, or actor during his childhood, although he did play drums. Talking about his early years, Cory says that he was a good student before the divorce. In kindergarten he was reading at a fourth-grade level and taking encyclopedias to bed with him. Yet he soon found himself in trouble.

Bad Boy

"I didn't have any definition of self," he told *Parade* magazine. "I never fit in, so I started pretending I was other people. I'd find people I thought were cool and dress how they dressed, talk how they talked, do whatever they were into."

By the age of thirteen, he was drinking and smoking pot. He transferred to new schools and got kicked out of others. By the time he dropped out of school for good at sixteen, he had attended twelve separate schools.

Time in rehab (a program to get sober) was no help for Cory. Like many addicts, it took a rock-bottom moment to examine whether he was going to continue on a destructive path or pull himself up and do something constructive with his life. "I stole a significant amount of money from a family member," he admits. "I knew I was going to get caught, but I was so desperate I didn't care. It was a cry for help. I was confronted and I said, 'Yeah, it was me.' It was the first honorable, truthful thing that had come out of my mouth in years."

The family member told him to quit drugs or he would report Cory to the police for theft. Cory decided he was tired of fighting himself. It was time to make changes. He moved to a small British Columbian city called Nanaimo. There, he got clean, surrounded himself with sober friends, and took back control of his life.

Getting Clean

Over the next few years, Cory took jobs as a Wal-Mart greeter, school bus driver, telemarketer, roofer, drummer in a local band, and taxi driver. One day a passenger in his cab suggested he try acting lessons with a coach he knew.

At this point, Cory was twenty, and the coach to whom he was introduced changed his life. Acting coach Andrew McIlroy taught a class in Nanaimo on weekends. Cory signed up. About three weeks in, McIlroy asked Cory to read a scene with him. Cory played the part of a man contemplating suicide. Afterward, McIlroy told him that he really had talent and could maybe make a living from acting. Cory says, "He's the reason I'm doing this. He was the guy that basically said to me, 'I think you can be an actor. I think you have that natural thing or whatever it is you need to have.' That's the only reason I started, literally. It was the first time somebody actually said that I was good at something. It was the first time I had ever been proficient at something."[22]

Hard Work Pays Off

That encouragement was exactly what Cory needed. He threw himself into acting with a passion. Just a few weeks after that first class, he moved to Vancouver, British Columbia, and started auditioning for roles. He credits McIlroy for not only teaching him about acting but also how to be a man and a decent human being.

Cory's mom, Ann, was also an influence. Cory says seeing how hard she worked to build her interior design business while raising him and his brother gave him a strong work ethic. Cory's agent, Elena Kirschner, agrees. She says Cory wasn't one of those kids who'd always dreamed of being an actor. "He came into acting backward. He didn't walk around with stars in his eyes," she says. "He always works his butt off. He's always prepared. It's not 'I wanna be a movie star.'"

Cory waited tables at night and took acting classes and attended auditions during the day. He moved from walk-on roles to larger roles in made-for-TV sci-fi movies. He also made guest appearances on TV shows such as *Smallville, Supernatural, Stargate SG-1, Flash Gordon*, and *Interns*. In 2006 he landed a recurring role in the TV series *Kyle XY* and then was cast as an ex-boyfriend-drummer on the MTV drama *Kaya*.

It was his drumming skills that helped Cory land his role on *Glee*. Producer Ryan Murphy had been looking for the standout triple threats–actors who can sing and dance. But after looking at hundreds of tapes, Murphy and his crew hadn't found the right combination of naïveté and sweetness that they wanted for the football jock character of Finn.

Cory's agent, Elena, wanted to show that Cory had musicality. So she sent a tape of Cory drumming with pencils on Tupperware, mugs, and wine glasses. It was goofy enough to get the producers' attention

Drum: Cory plays the drums at a Canadian awards gala in 2010. His drumming ability played a part in getting him an audition for *Glee*.

but not compelling enough for them to spring for airfare. Cory drove more than twenty hours from Vancouver to Los Angeles to sing in front of them. On the way, he practiced to *Billy Joel's Greatest Hits* and the *Rent* sound track. He chose the Billy Joel ballad "Honesty" to sing for Ryan Murphy and *Glee*'s casting director. In fact, this was the first time Cory had ever sung in front of an audience! A few days later, he and two other actors were called back to audition for Fox executives. Thirty minutes later, Cory got a call from his agent and his manager. He had the part!

Character Building

Cory's acting skills are so strong that even though he's at least ten years older than the character he plays, he is still completely believable as dim-witted but earnest high schooler Finn Hudson. In 2009 Cory was nominated for Teen Choice's TV Breakout Star: Male award. That year also brought an important event to Cory's life. After speaking only about four times to his father since his parents' divorce, Cory's dad contacted him through Facebook. They arranged a visit. When Joe and his wife, Yvette, picked Cory up

Tall talent: Cory wears his trademark football jersey in a scene with Lea's Rachel. The off-and-on romance between Cory's Finn and Lea's Rachel is central to the show.

from the airport, they were so excited and proud they were in tears. "At some point, you realize your parents are human," says Cory. "They make the best decisions they can with the options available to them."

In 2011 Cory cohosted the Teen Choice Awards and won the Choice TV Actor: Comedy award. On top of that, he also earned a Screen Actors Guild (SAG) award for Outstanding Performance by an Ensemble in a Comedy Series. Cory also made his major feature film debut in 2011 in the movie *Monte Carlo.* He played Owen, a young man in love with Selena Gomez's character, Grace. Because his part was relatively minor, he was able to travel throughout Europe during filming.

Choice for teens: Cory not only hosted the Teen Choice Awards in 2011; he also won the award for Choice TV Actor: Comedy. He is shown here with the surfboard winners receive at the show.

He went to airports and train stations and randomly picked places to go. He would love to do more travel and more feature films.

To help people who feel they have limited options, Cory has teamed with Sir Richard Branson's nonprofit foundation Virgin Unite on their RE*Generation program, which targets at-risk youths. A former at-risk youth himself, Cory works with groups that give homeless young people in Canada a chance to turn their lives around, get off the streets, and move toward a better future.

Life after *Glee*

A proud Canadian, Cory is a huge fan of hockey (favorite team: the Canucks). He also loves basketball, skimboarding, surfing, and *Guitar Hero II*. In 2011 he joined some friends to form the band Bonnie Dune, named after a utopian place in the Australian movie *The Castle*. Also in 2011, Cory received a high school diploma from one of the high schools he had attended in Victoria. The school gave him the diploma based on "abilities demonstrated in the workplace."

As for life after Finn graduates from McKinley, Cory remains optimistic for continued movie and TV opportunities. He believes if he keeps showing up, working hard, and doing his best, things will fall into place in the future, just as they have in the past.

CHAPTER THREE

The bad boy and the diva: Mark Salling (*left*) and Amber Riley (*right*) play Noah "Puck" Puckerman and Mercedes Jones on *Glee*. Their characters dated briefly in a season 1 episode.

Amber Riley and Mark Salling

■■■■■

Amber Riley hates auditions. But she was excited about this one. Ever since she was two years old, everyone had told her she was a great singer. She'd sung at her church as a kid. When she got older, she sang backup in clubs around her hometown of Los Angeles with family and friends. She had the voice. She just had to overcome her nerves. On this cold San Francisco day, she waited in her sleeping bag outside on the concrete. As she got closer to the front of the line, she started to feel anxious. She felt so panicked she didn't think she could walk. She sang for the producers, they shook their heads. It was a no.

Amber was devastated. These were industry people. They knew what they were talking about. Was it possible they were right? That singing wasn't her thing? She cried harder than she'd ever cried in her life. During the seven-hour car ride home, Amber's parents consoled her. Don't give up. This will make you stronger. "It was a very humbling experience after being told how good I was the whole time," says Amber about being rejected by *American Idol*. "My mom said, 'You know what you have and you know who you are and you know the gift you have. You just have to work harder.'"

Back in Los Angeles, Amber concentrated on school, graduating from La Mirada High School in 2004. She took a job as a customer service rep at IKEA and loved it. She also worked hard on singing and overcoming her nerves. At various auditions though, she was told she was a little too big or not the look they were after. It made her determined to work harder. She quit her job and focused full-time on music. Soon after that, she attended the audition that would turn out to be a yes—the role of Mercedes Jones on *Glee*.

The right fit: Amber had lots of disappointing auditioning experiences before finding the role that was perfect for her—Mercedes on *Glee*.

The Family Business

Amber Patrice Riley was born on February 15, 1986, to Tiny and Elwin Riley. She joined a family with two girls, Ashley and Toiya. Tiny was a gospel singer, and before Amber started kindergarten, she joined her mother singing in the choir at church. Her mom insisted on vocal training and encouraged acting lessons because she thought it might help Amber break into the music industry. Amber's whole family consisted of actors, dancers, writers, and others working in creative fields. It wasn't much of a surprise to see young Amber dancing, singing, or acting in plays. She admits she was quite the drama queen growing up.

At sixteen she was cast in a pilot called *St. Sass*. While the show never aired, it did allow her to meet its producer—a young man named Ryan Murphy. But before she'd meet Ryan again, there was high school to get through. Amber was involved in gospel choir, drama club, and theater. She took dance, jazz, and opera classes. Her friends gave her the nickname Hollywood, claiming one day she'd be famous. She

Proud mother: Amber and her mother, Tiny Riley, arrive at the NAACP Image Awards in 2011. Amber was nominated for Outstanding Supporting Actress in a Comedy Series.

dated a little in high school but was mainly focused on activities that would help an entertainment career. She laughs, "My parents were like, 'It's nice to have a boyfriend, but it's even *nicer* to own your house when you're 21.'"

More Than Her Dress Size

After *St. Sass*, Amber took a break from auditions. The constant rejection was affecting her self-esteem. She had to remind herself that she was not her dress size. She was Amber Riley, with a unique gift and talent. And if she didn't look like the typical industry star, then she would just work all the harder. In 2008 she was ready to audition again. She had heard through a friend of a friend about a casting director who was looking for a black girl singer who could really belt it out. While she didn't consider herself a belter, she thought she'd give it a try. She was surprised when she arrived at the audition to find that what she'd thought was a singing audition was also an acting audition. The role she'd thought was a background character was one of the principal players. Even so, she was calm. She figured that if she got the role, great. But if she didn't, she was still going to pursue her dream.

The next surprise was a pleasant one—seeing Ryan Murphy's name on the script. Ryan told her that the character of Mercedes was a diva and that Amber needed to forget her natural sweetness and politeness and be the opposite of who she was. She went for it, giving a powerhouse rendition of "And I Am Telling You I'm Not Going" from the movie *Dreamgirls*. Soon afterward, she received the news. She was to play Mercedes Jones on the new show *Glee*!

Celebrity Role Model

Amber describes the next year as a whirlwind. One week she was nominated for Female Scene Stealer for the Teen Choice Awards. Then she won as part of the *Glee* cast in Outstanding Performance by an Ensemble in a Comedy Series at the SAG Awards. Another week the cast got to meet Oprah and appeared on the *Oprah Winfrey Show*. Not long after, Amber sang the national anthem at Major League Baseball's All-Star Game. It was enough to go to anyone's head, but Amber remained grounded.

She says "As a celebrity you have two choices—you can either be a celebrity, or you can choose to be a role model, and I feel like we have chosen to be role models. The letters that we get are so touching, and so honest and open with us, I feel the obligation to be the same exact way with [fans]. I feel like a lot of us are different—

All-Star singer: Amber sings the national anthem at baseball's All-Star Game in Anaheim, California, in July 2010.

we don't look like the typical stars that you see in Hollywood, and for us to be that example and be so big to [fans] . . . It's empowering for them and it's empowering for us."

Plus-Sized Mentor

Amber was especially embraced by plus-sized girls. She says she loves inspiring girls to be comfortable with their bodies. She also joined a beauty brand's campaign against bullying called Mean Stinks. The interactive Facebook site provides access to experts, tools, resources, and tips for dealing with bullies or with being a bully. Amber's advice includes being proactive. Tell an adult or someone who can help with the situation, rather than trying to fight back with words alone.

December 30, 2010

Big is beautiful: Not all good news

From the Pages of
USA TODAY

Remember the "black is beautiful" movement? Well, now the "big is beautiful" image is in—and the heavy-set crowd is finding acceptance.

For decades, Oprah Winfrey has represented the plus-size woman on best-dressed lists. Now MTV's "Twitter Jockey" Gabi Gregg, who also edits the blog *Young, Fat and Fabulous*, is making big-girl style her business. Gregg isn't alone in the fato-sphere. Earlier this year, *Vogue Italia* launched the website Vogue Curvy, featuring plus-size models in couture fashions.

But can too much of a positive self-perception be unhealthy? Especially when some of us should be making New Year's resolutions to start losing weight?

A study published in the December issue of *Obstetrics & Gynecology* found that 23% of overweight women saw themselves as being smaller than they were. The misperception was especially acute for black and Latina women. The study found that more than 80% of African-American women and 75% of Hispanic-American women were overweight or obese, and were less likely than white women to see themselves as overweight. (If your body mass index is over 25, you are considered overweight, and if over 30, obese.)

The study was headed by Abbey Berenson, a researcher at the University of Texas Medical Branch in Galveston, and looked at more than 2,200 women. The survey participants tended to be low-income. Researchers noted that overweight women who see themselves as normal weight are less likely to try and lose weight.

The researchers also warned that misperceptions about one's weight could lead women to eat poorly, gain more weight and, as a result, develop complications from obesity, including diabetes and hypertension. Denial should not be confused with high self-esteem, especially when it risks our health.

I'm reminded of the confident and rotund Mercedes played by Amber Riley on Fox's show *Glee*. In one episode, she scoffs at the idea of losing weight. On another she defiantly demands to have the greasy Tater Tots returned to the lunch menu.

Mercedes and other obese women must face the music: If obesity becomes more socially acceptable, the dangers to their health could all too easily be overlooked.

—Yolanda Young, founder of www.onbeingablacklawyer.com

For girls who are miserable in high school, she stresses that high school is only four years and that life after high school rocks. She urges young women to stand up for one another and to speak up when they see others in a bad situation.

Working fourteen- to sixteen-hour days on *Glee* can be exhausting. But Amber is known for her warm, mothering manner. Her nickname Mama Amber or Mama A comes from looking out for the others in the cast. Like many of the other actors, she considers the *Glee* cast and crew her family away from home. She says that the First Wives Club—where the girls get together in Lea Michele's on-set trailer—is a great

Mama Amber: *Glee* costars Chord Overstreet (who plays Sam Evans) and Amber pose for a photo at a premiere in 2011. Amber is close to many members of the *Glee* cast.

Star-spangled song: Amber sings the national anthem for President Barack Obama and his family during the White House Easter Egg Roll in 2010.

way to relax and blow off steam. So is hanging out at Cory's house (because it's the biggest) or going out for sushi together. Like many of the cast, Amber has tattoos. On her wrist, she has the logo of the Christian clothing company Not of This World. On her back, she has a bird tattoo because her family calls her Songbird.

Achieving Her Dreams

Amber says her most nerve-racking experience to date was singing the national anthem at the White House in 2010. She was so nervous she felt as if she was going to throw up and kept repeating to herself "Don't forget the words ... don't forget the words. ..." Her cast mates had assured her she'd be great and that if she was really nervous, she should just look down at them in the audience below. When she did, she saw that they were so proud of her they had tears running down their faces. Not helping!!

Looking back afterward, Amber remembered a "bucket list" she'd made in high school: meet the president, meet Oprah, and attend the Grammys (the Grammy Award ceremony recognizes outstanding achievement in the music industry). As part of the *Glee* phenomenon, she'd achieved them all before she was twenty-four. Reflecting on her journey, Amber wonders whether she would have gotten to where she is if it had not been for the *American Idol* rejection.

"I am really glad they told me no, because maybe if they hadn't, I

USA TODAY Snapshots®

Activities we'd put on our bucket list

Drive a race car	34%
Ride a motorcycle	29%
Sky-dive	28%
Run a marathon	23%
Bungee jump	18%

Source: BMW survey of 1,000 adults by Wakefield Research

By Michelle Healy and Sam Ward, USA TODAY, 2010

never would have strived for my full potential or reached my full potential. I might have rested on my laurels," she says, offering advice to others striving to make their dreams come true. "The best advice I can give is just be focused, be sure about what you want and don't let anyone tell you no, you can't do it. Don't let that deter you."

Mark Salling—Music Man

It's hard to believe that Mark Salling, who plays Noah "Puck" Puckerman, was ever ready to give up. But he didn't get to stardom overnight. He spent seven years in Los Angeles, trying to catch a break in the music industry. The CD he released under the name Jericho hadn't really gone anywhere, even though he'd put his heart and soul into it. He played all the instruments, wrote all the songs, sang, and even produced the tracks. He played in some Los Angeles bars that didn't exactly pay the rent. So he earned extra money giving guitar lessons. But living paycheck to paycheck was becoming exhausting. Was it time to

Young musician: Mark, shown here in an eighth-grade portrait, could play three instruments by the time he entered junior high school.

give up his pipe dreams, go home, and get a "real" job?

Things had seemed much easier in Dallas, Texas, where Mark had grown up. He was born on August 17, 1982, to Condy, a secretary, and John, an accountant. Mark Wayne Salling was the younger of the couple's two children, joining his older brother, Matt, in a strict, Christian family. After being homeschooled for a while, he attended Providence Christian School and Our Redeemer Lutheran School. He started piano lessons at the age of five (inspired by the 1984 movie *Amadeus* about Wolfgang Amadeus Mozart, a genius musician and composer of classical music). By the time Mark reached junior high school, he could play guitar, bass, and drums. He took acting classes at the Dallas Children's Theater and at the age of eleven was cast in a beer commercial. At thirteen he was cast as Naomi Watt's son in the movie *Children of the Corn IV: The Gathering*, which was being shot in his hometown. He then had a guest role on the TV show *Walker, Texas Ranger* and a part in *The Graveyard*, an indie horror film, both filmed in Dallas.

As a high school junior and senior, Mark took part in his school's variety show. He also showcased his musical talents in a cover band at a local bar. These early successes encouraged him to pursue an entertainment career. He headed to California and attended the Los Angeles

Music Academy in Pasadena, California. But the musical dreams he had never seemed to pan out. He considered moving to Austin, Texas. It has a strong music scene, and he thought maybe things would pick up there. But first he had a heart-to-heart phone conversation with his brother, Matt. The call inspired him to lift his game to the highest level. He put together one hundred packets containing head shots and his résumé. He sent them to fifty managers and fifty agents he'd found on LAcasting.com.

Mohawk madness: Mark wore his hair in a Mohawk hairstyle for his audition for Puck. The character would continue with the look for much of the first three seasons.

Getting His Break

Just one person responded, but that one manager introduced him to an agent. The agent sent Mark on an audition for a TV pilot in a role as a "bad boy." He decided to wear his hair in a Mohawk as a way to stand out from the other actors. "I hadn't been on an audition in years, I had to sing in a roomful of strangers at nine in the morning," Mark said. "It was intimidating, to say the least, but it was my best audition ever."

Four more auditions later, Mark was cast as *Glee*'s Noah "Puck" Puckerman, the jock

Side project: *(Left to right)* Mark, Ashley Fink, and *Glee* casting director Robert Ulrich talk to contenstants on an episode of *The Glee Project*. In this show, contestants competed to appear on season 3 of *Glee*. Cast members such as Mark and Ashley (who played Lauren Zizes on the first two seasons of *Glee*) gave performance advice to contestants.

football player who throws kids into school Dumpsters, impregnates head cheerleader Quinn, puts weed in the bake sale cupcakes, spends time in juvie, and initially starts singing just to attract older women. Despite the bad boy credentials, the character of Puck soon revealed a softer side. Mark says one of the challenges he faces is "making the character more than two-dimensional. . . . He has to be a jerk and be likeable at the same time. I had to make him likeable so I had to find the balance between arrogance and cocky and sensible and likeable."

Season 2 offered Puck a chance to show off his less shallow side through the story line he shared with Lauren Zizes (played by Ashley Fink). Although she has the hefty physique of a champion wrestler, Puck is attracted to her confident swagger. Ashley explains the attraction as a certain tough-chick chemistry.

Big Hearted

In real life, Mark shares few similarities with his on-screen character. "I've never thrown anyone into a Dumpster, for one thing," he says, laughing. "I was a wrestler, not a football player. And I haven't broken *that* many hearts—I've only had two serious girlfriends." He's also been able to use his fame to give a voice to causes close to his heart. These include campaigns to raise money for school music programs and end child hunger. "Child hunger is something we think of as a foreign issue and it's a huge issue right here in the United States." He says that "17 million kids are affected. Actually, my native state of Texas is number two on that list, so I feel a personal connection."

Mark also donates his time to another cause that's close to his heart—birds. He volunteers with the James Hunter Wildlife Rescue charity in Burbank, California. He regularly posts links to bird photos from his Twitter account. He can often be found on the set of *Glee* sketching pictures of birds and nature. Off the set, he likes playing

Inspiring others: Mark performs with students during a visit to a middle school in Los Angeles in 2011. He visited the school as part of a VH-1 Save the Music event. The organization donated instruments to the school's music program.

basketball, Frisbee golf, lifting weights at the gym, and going out for sushi with friends—often his *Glee* cast mates. He says his vices are hamburgers and beautiful women.

During *Glee*'s first season, Mark was seen making out with costar Naya Rivera at *Glee*'s spring premiere. Both denied they were in a relationship, claiming they're just good friends. She does fit his type, though. Mark says, "I usually go for the ethnic ladies. That's kinda my preference, but I don't discriminate."

Pipe Dreams

He's equally eclectic in his music tastes, listing '90s grunge such as Alice in Chains, Nirvana, and Pearl Jam with Nine Inch Nails, Radiohead, Led Zeppelin, Elliot Smith, Rufus Wainwright, country, and jazz as some of his favorite music and biggest influences. It was those influences that Mark wove into his 2010 solo CD. Mark produced the disc and released it under his own label. The tracks reveal some topics dear to him, including religion, Alzheimer's, and children's books. The CD and record label share the same name—Pipe Dreams. "Pipe dreams is a term that represents what people will tell you are unrealistic dreams," says Mark, reflecting on his own ambitions as a teen. "That's kind of what me considering a career in music and moving out west was—a pipe dream."

These days, as a breakout star on a hugely popular TV series, Mark seems to have achieved success beyond his wildest dreams. He is glad he didn't give up. When asked to what one person he owes his success, this so-called bad boy gives a very un-Puck like answer: "My grandma."

CHAPTER FOUR

Singing and dancing: Jenna Ushkowitz (*left*) and Harry Shum Jr. (*right*) are all dressed up for the Golden Globe Awards in January 2012. Both actors have had dancing on their résumés since they were young children. Their characters have been dating on the show since season 2.

Jenna Ushkowitz
and
Harry Shum Jr.

Lea Michele might have the nickname Child Star, but there's another member of the *Glee* cast who has been in show business even longer. Jenna Noelle Ushkowitz— who plays Tina Cohen-Chang—got her show biz start at the age of three. She was in print and TV commercials before moving to TV and Broadway.

Jenna was born on April 28, 1986, in Seoul, South Korea. When she was three months old, she was adopted by an American family living in Long Island, New York. Her Polish last name comes from her father, who has a Polish Italian background. Her mother is Irish English. Jenna was so outgoing as a toddler that friends and even strangers suggested to her parents she should be on the stage. So they found a manager on Long Island. Jenna was quickly cast in TV ads.

Broadway Baby

Jenna graduated from commercials to TV shows, appearing on *Sesame Street*, *Reading Rainbow*, and *As the World Turns*. While still in elementary school, she auditioned for and won a role on the 1996 Broadway revival of the classic musical *The King and I*. This ignited her love of live theater.

"I've loved music for as long as I can remember," says Jenna. "I always did summer theater, but I think I really got to understand what the lifestyle was like when I did *The King and I* on Broadway at the age of 9. It was a big responsibility for a 9-year-old, but I couldn't wait to get to the theater to perform for a live audience and see my new family every day. It was then that I decided I wanted to pursue it."

Ready for the stage: Young Jenna shows off some dance moves. By the age of nine, Jenna was appearing in her first Broadway show.

It was around this time that Jenna met Lea Michele, who was performing in *Ragtime*. They had seen each other at a number of Broadway auditions and were introduced by a mutual friend. Lea attended Jenna's birthday party. The two girls and a friend would talk by three-way calling, which was popular at the time.

As a young person, Jenna took voice, dance, and acting classes. On weekends she performed in a show Off-Broadway with a group called the Broadway Kids. In this show, kids from eight to fourteen with Broadway experience perform songs from Broadway musicals. When she was just thirteen, Jenna sang the national anthem live in front of a huge crowd at a New York Knicks basketball game at Madison Square Garden.

Gleeful experience: Jenna, shown in her senior picture, had a great time in high school. She was part of many groups, including her school's glee club.

Overachiever

Jenna attended Holy Trinity Diocesan High School, a performing arts Catholic high school on Long Island. She describes herself back then as a type A overachiever. She was class president, a member of the student council, and vice president of the school's glee club. She says she had a great time in high school. Her bubbly, friendly personality allowed her to mix with all her classmates.

In school plays, Jenna played Penny in *Honk!* Inez in *The Baker's Wife*, and Romaine Patterson in *The Laramie Project*. Dance and acting classes were every day, with voice lessons once a week. "We all performed," she says. "There was lots of crying, singing and dancing through the halls. You had people singing for you, breaking into song every few minutes, from high school through college."

Confidence Is King

While she was full of confidence onstage, Jenna could be nervous in other areas. She failed the road test for her driver's license twice before passing on her third attempt. She remembers that she was so nervous behind the wheel that she could hardly pull out into the street. At seventeen she took a summer job at the bagel shop of a friend's uncle, working three days a week. Although she loved eating bagels (she still does!), after two months she'd had enough of the long hours and smelling like bagels all the time. She was so anxious about offending the owner that she needed her mother's help to quit the job.

Jenna went to Marymount Manhattan College, where she graduated in three years (2007) with a bachelor's degree in acting and a minor in musical theater. In her freshman year of college, she played the role of Little Red iding Hood in *Into the Woods*, a part she had also played in her senior year of high school.

After graduating from college, Jenna didn't slow down.

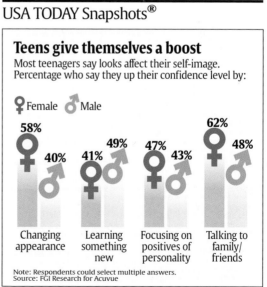

USA TODAY Snapshots®

Teens give themselves a boost

Most teenagers say looks affect their self-image.
Percentage who say they up their confidence level by:

♀ Female ♂ Male

	Changing appearance	Learning something new	Focusing on positives of personality	Talking to family/ friends
Female	58%	41%	47%	62%
Male	40%	49%	43%	48%

Note: Respondents could select multiple answers.
Source: FGI Research for Acuvue

By Rebecca F. Johnson and Alejandro Gonzalez, USA TODAY, 2007

She joined the cast of Broadway's *Spring Awakening*. In this play, she was "swing" for several parts including Thea, Martha, and Anna. Swings are understudies (backup actors and singers) for the chorus. They need to be familiar with all the dances for all their characters and keep the parts straight in their head. Jenna also was the understudy for the part of Ilse in *Spring Awakening*. Jenna joined the cast just as Lea was leaving. She says Lea was super welcoming and introduced her to the cast. Having lost touch during the busy high school years, Jenna says it was really nice to connect with Lea again as adults.

 A swing is an understudy of a dance chorus line. Swings are people who know the chorus routines perfectly. Regular chorus members don't all perform the exact same dance moves at the same time. Sometimes they are split in half, and each side mirrors the moves of the other side. A swing can replace any chorus member, no matter where that person dances in the line. But ask a regular chorus member to switch places, and that person is bound to mess up because he or she has perfected it from only one side.

The Time of Her Life

The casting director of *Spring Awakening*, Jim Carnahan, was also the New York casting associate for *Glee*. Looking for promising talent for the show, he had some of his cast, including Jenna, read for parts. He sent the videotape to Ryan Murphy and Brad Falchuk. Both were impressed with Jenna's talent. More readings and auditions followed be

Friends again: Jenna *(left)* and Lea *(right)* were happy to work together again when they were cast in *Glee*. They first met when both were in Broadway shows as children and then again when Jenna joined the cast of *Spring Awakening*. Here they are performing during one of the *Glee Live!* concerts in May 2011.

fore Jenna got the call. She had the part of Tina Cohen-Chang!

Like the rest of the cast, Jenna describes the first couple of seasons of *Glee* as a tumultuous blend of long hours, tours, and promotions. But the rewards are worth it. "We are one big happy family. Cast and crew," she says. "We have amazing, talented people surrounding us every day and it's a fresh, positive, creative atmosphere where people are always laughing and having a good time. Sure, it's tedious and there are long hours, but that's the nitty gritty and that's my favorite part.

"If we aren't shooting, we are rehearsing in the dance studio and if we aren't doing that, we are in the recording studio. An episode takes 8 days and our days are pretty long, usually around 12 hours. But there are so many of us and we are all around the same age, so we are always hanging out together." Although Jenna misses the energy of live

Back to the city: Jenna *(right center in green coat)* and the rest of the female cast members of *Glee* film a scene in New York City for the second season finale in 2011. Fans can be seen in the background watching the filming.

audiences and hopes to get back to Broadway someday, she says she's having the time of her life on the show right now. During the filming of the season 2 finale in New York City in 2011, she practically had to pinch herself.

"We thought we would go shoot and a couple of fans would be there. It was insane. Hundreds and hundreds of kids showed up. There were barricades everywhere. It was overwhelming, amazing and kind of wakes you up, going, [wow], this is my life now!"

Harry Shum Jr.—Daring to Be Different

When Harry Shum Jr. was very young, his parents took him to a therapist. "He's so shy!" they told her. "He rarely speaks!" This shy, quiet kid eventually emerged from his shell to create a career onstage. He's been a backup dancer on tour with Beyoncé, Mariah Carey, and Jennifer Lopez, among others. And he is in front of the camera on *Glee* as the character Mike Chang. At first, though, Harry's traditional parents were not very excited about their son's choice of careers.

Harry's dad was born in Fujian, China, and his mom was born in Hong Kong. In the 1970s, they moved to Costa Rica in Central America to start a new business. Harry Jr. was born on April 28, 1982, in Puerto Limón, joining two older sisters, Cristina and Susana. The whole family spoke Spanish, the local language. When Harry was five, his family moved to San Francisco where Harry learned English and Cantonese.

Dance fever: Harry *(second from right)* and other male cast members perform a musical number during *Glee*'s second season. Harry and his character Mike Chang are both known for their dancing skills.

Dancing Props

Harry didn't dance until he was in high school and then only because of a dare. He'd participated in school plays since middle school. He was also busy with track and field, pole vaulting, tennis, relay races, and debating. After seeing the school dance team perform, Harry was captivated by how joyful the dancers looked onstage. His track-and-field buddies dared him to join and he did.

Harry was disappointed that the male members of the team were treated as props rather than as dancers. So he started choreographing routines that would allow the boys to shine. A few screaming girls later, the dance team became a cool gig. Jocks and football players clamored to join. Harry started dance training in earnest, spending hours watching music videos and copying the moves of Ginuwine, Dru Hill, Usher, Janet Jackson, the Backstreet Boys, and 'N Sync. Once he'd figured out those moves, he moved on to those of dance legends Michael Jackson and Gene Kelly.

As many parents do, Harry's parents wanted him to finish college and have a stable career—as a doctor or a dentist perhaps. He enrolled in San Francisco State University studying cinema—his passion—and international business, to please his parents. While there he also took classes at Dance Mission Theater with Jesse Santos, a Los Angeles-based dancer who had danced with Pink and Michael Jackson. After seeing that Jesse was making a living as a dancer, Harry decided to postpone university studies and move to Los Angeles. He bought unlimited class passes to Millennium Dance Complex, Edge Performing Arts Center, and the Debbie Reynolds Studio, practically living at the studios.

Getting Noticed

It wasn't long before his natural athleticism and grace were noticed by choreographers, and he was invited to join a tour in the United Kingdom with pop singer Kaci. "It was an awesome experience," Harry says, "especially for an 18-year-old kid who was completely new to the industry." That tour led to others. Over the next six years, Harry traveled the world with Destiny's Child, Beyoncé, Jessica Simpson, Mariah Carey, Ashanti, T-Pain, and Chris Brown, among others.

Back stateside, Harry was cast in one of the first iPod commercials, featuring the dancing silhouettes. A huge Apple fan, Harry was thrilled when the company called him back for several more ads including the launch of the iPod Nano in 2005.

Putting some of his focus into his first love, acting, Harry auditioned for various films and TV shows. He got small roles in *Boston Public, You Got Served, Stomp the Yard, Zoey 101,* and *iCarly.* In 2008 he was cast as Cable in the dance movie *Step Up 2: The Streets* (a role he played again in *Step Up 3D*). It was on the set of *Step Up 2* that he met director Jon M. Chu. The two teamed up together to form *The LXD* (*The Legion of Extraordinary Dancers*), an online series depicting dancers as superheroes and villains. *The LXD* came to the attention of the producers of TV's *So You Think You Can Dance*. A featured LXD routine on that show was followed by performances at a 2010 TED (Technology Entertainment and Design) conference in front of former vice president Al Gore and Microsoft founder Bill Gates. That, in turn, led to Harry co-choreographing an LXD routine for the 82nd Annual Academy Awards in March 2010.

While filming and choreographing *The LXD* episodes for online distribution, Harry auditioned for an unnamed role on a show to be called *Glee*. He was originally hired as a day player (a supporting actor paid on a daily basis without a long-term contract). He was then asked to stay for nine weeks. Originally billed as "the Other Asian," Harry's portrayal

They are legion: Cast and crew of *The Legion of Extraordinary Dancers (LXD)* celebrate at the Web series premiere in 2010. Harry *(right center in black coat and tie)* and other *LXD* members were the opening act on both *Glee Live!* concert tours.

of mainly silent Mike Chang was reminiscent of the young, quiet Harry Jr. Although he didn't have many lines, he captured hearts anyway. The nine weeks turned into two years. Harry's recurring guest role was officially changed to "series regular" for season 3. Where season 2 dealt mainly with Mike's relationship with his girlfriend Tina, season 3 includes an episode exploring more of Mike's character's background, including his family.

Smooth moves: Harry and other cast members perform during the *Glee: The 3D Concert Movie* in 2011. Harry sports a shirt that says "Can't Sing," but his character began singing in addition to dancing in season 3.

Parents on Board

And speaking of family, Harry's formerly cautious and concerned parents are now his biggest supporters. He comments, "Traditional Asian/Chinese parents, they don't really know this world—the entertainment world; that you can actually—if you do it right—can actually make a good living and you know, go on and live a good life. . . . It took them watching a few times . . . but now I have their full support."

And what would Harry pass on to his kids that he learned from his parents? "I'm still very involved with my cultural background in the sense that I speak Chinese and still learn from my mom about how to cook ethnic foods, my heritage, and how things are done. Of course, I live in America; my main culture's here, so I want to keep a balance. I don't want to lose one or the other; I want them to merge. It's very important to me that when I have kids, they learn about Chinese culture and speak Chinese. To pass this on to my kids and their kids' kids as my parents did with me is really important to me."

'Step Up' movies feed off dance fever

From the Pages of
USA TODAY

Harry Shum Jr.

Role: Born in Costa Rica and raised in California, Shum, 28, reprises his *Step Up 2 the Streets* character, Cable, one of the Maryland School of the Arts grads who help out the Pirates.

Dance dues: This freestyler is at the epicenter of the current dance-quake. Shum has choreographed for *So You Think You Can Dance*, plays jock turned choir boy Mike Chang on Fox's *Glee* and is a co-choreographer and member of the *Legion of Extraordinary Dancers*. He got his start on his high school's dance team. "I wasn't very good. I don't know how I got on the team. I think I spun a couple times. I was a goofball. But as a technician, I slowly tried to figure things out and see how they worked."

It's all relative: Shum never met [director Jon M.] Chu before *Step Up 2*. But turns out he could have asked the director's father for a reference—along with the bill. "His dad owns a popular restaurant in Palo Alto [California]. I told him, 'Oh, I ate at your dad's restaurant all the time.'"

—Susan Wloszczyna

Extraordinary collaboration: Director Jon M. Chu *(left)* and Harry *(right)* met filming *Step Up 2* in 2008 and followed up the movie with *LXD*, an online dance show.

Fan favorites: Naya Rivera *(left)*, Heather Morris *(center)*, and Kevin McHale posed for photos with fans when the cast was on location in New York City in April 2011.

Kevin McHale, Heather Morris, and Naya Rivera

■■■■■

Even as a small child, Kevin Michael McHale—who plays Artie—knew what he wanted to be. Born June 14, 1988, and growing up with three much older siblings in Plano, Texas, he desperately wanted to be an entertainer. His parents, Elizabeth and Christopher, recall that when people asked his name, Kevin would say it was Michael Jackson. His other obsession back then was with the hit musical *The Lion King*. In fact, if you Google "Kevin McHale Lion King," you'll come across the home movie of Kevin's first public performance—singing "I Just Can't Wait to Be King." Kevin sang this song from *The Lion King* at his sister Shannon's wedding when he was only six years old. Years later, Shannon gave the footage to Jay Leno to play as a surprise for Kevin's 2010 appearance on Leno's late-night talk show *The Tonight Show*.

Family connection: Kevin chats with Jay Leno during his 2010 appearance on *The Tonight Show*. Kevin's sister once worked for Leno. She gave the show a recording of six-year-old Kevin singing, which aired during his Leno visit.

Boy Band Beginnings

Shannon used to work for Leno. When she left *The Tonight Show with Jay Leno* in 1996, she became a talent agent. This opened some doors for Kevin to audition for local TV commercials. It also helped him line up singing opportunities at malls in Dallas, Texas, with another Texas native—Demi Lovato. In 2003, when Kevin was fourteen, he joined the boy band NLT (Not Like Them), a reference to other boy bands of that time.

With Shannon and Kevin's two older brothers, Chris and Tim, grown up and out of the home, Kevin and his parents moved to Los Angeles to help his career. He booked some small parts in TV shows including *The Office*. On this show, he played a pizza delivery boy who is kidnapped by Dwight (Rainn Wilson) and Michael (Steve Carell) when he refuses to honor a coupon. Kevin attended school in Los Angeles but kept his professional life separate, not joining in acting or singing classes at school.

In 2007 NLT signed a record deal with Geffen Records. NLT had the opportunity to collaborate with top producers and songwriters including Pharrell, Ne-Yo, and Timbaland. The same year, the group also joined the Pussycat Dolls on tour as their opening act. NLT released a debut single called "She Said, I Said (Time We Let Go)," which was a 2007 Top 40 hit. They released other singles after that, but an album never came together.

In 2008 Kevin landed a recurring role of Dooley on *Zoey 101* and a brief two-episode run on *True Blood*. NLT went on tour with V

Not Like Them: Kevin *(second from right)* and the other members of NLT pose backstage at MTV in 2008. The band toured and put out singles but never released an album.

Factory and Menudo as headliners in a House of Blues Tour, the 2009 Bandemonium Tour. But eventually, without an album to promote, the band broke up.

It must have been fate that casting for *Glee* took place that same year as the Bandemonium Tour. Kevin knew immediately when he read the script that he wanted to be a part of the show. Like many of his cast mates, he loved to sing and dance as well as act. The show would give him the chance to do all three. He laughed out loud reading the script, something no other script had done for him.

Setting the Wheels in Motion

As a seasoned performer, Kevin found the audition process for *Glee* to be relatively easy. He sang "Let It Be" by the Beatles, a song he loves so much he has the title tattooed on his wrist. The hard part was waiting six weeks after the auditioning before learning he had the part.

Keep rolling: Kevin performs a Michael Jackson song during the *Glee: The 3D Concert Movie*. Kevin is an accomplished dancer. But when he's in character, he almost always performs in a wheelchair.

Kevin's cast mates all agree that Kevin is the best dancer. Yet he plays Artie, the student in a wheelchair, unable to dance. Kevin laughs it off, saying he's happy he gets to sit down all day while the others have to learn complicated dance routines. He did have his chance to shine though in episode 19, "Dream On." In a dream sequence during that episode, he dances to "Safety Dance" with a flash mob in a Los Angeles mall. In real life,

Kevin does learn some of the routines so he can stand in for other actors when necessary during rehearsals.

At promotional appearances, people are often surprised to find that Kevin is nondisabled. Many viewers believe his TV wheelchair life is real. All the same, they are thrilled to see his character attracting hot cheerleaders like Brittany and arty girls like Tina. Kevin claims he is much shyer with girls in his own life than the superconfident Artie. When pressed, he admits he likes arty, funky girls like Haley Williams from Paramore or exotic beauties like Nicole Scherzinger of the Pussycat Dolls.

Glee has Kevin doing things he'd never thought he'd be doing. This includes not only learning to use a wheelchair but also rapping and covering an extraordinary range of songs from blues to rock to show tunes. One of his favorite songs so far? It would have to be "P.Y.T. (Pretty Young Thing)" by Michael Jackson. Singing this song made his lifelong dream to be Michael Jackson come true. The episode dedicated to Jackson was icing on the cake. By achieving his dreams, Kevin will likely inspire a new generation of little boys to want to be the next Kevin McHale.

IN FOCUS

Peabody Awards

According to its website, the Peabody Awards "recognize distinguished achievement and meritorious service by broadcasters, cable and Webcasters, producing organizations, and individuals." *Glee* was awarded a Peabody Award in 2010 with the following description from the organization: "Dependably tuneful and entertaining, the musical dramedy that revolves around the motley members of a high-school choral club hit especially high notes with episodes such as 'Wheels,' about the daily struggles of a wheelchair-bound singer."

November 18, 2005

Access for disabled remains elusive

From the Pages of
USA TODAY
A Supreme Court decision on Monday seems to make equal education harder to obtain for special needs students. In *Schaffer v. Weast*, the Court ruled that parents have the burden of proving that the school system does not provide a free, appropriate education for their special needs child. This case reminds us how far we have come, and how much more work must be done, to secure equal rights for the 54 million disabled citizens in the USA.

The Individuals with Disabilities Education Improvement Act (IDEA) mandates equal educational opportunities for disabled kids. It requires public schools to provide education for special needs students, a disproportionate number of whom are African-American and Latino. If the Court's ruling allows school districts to pare [trim] special education budgets, and protects them from challenges, these kids will lose in the long run.

Adults with disabilities are less likely than those without disabilities to have finished high school or college. They are less likely to find employment and more likely to live in poverty. According to a 2004 survey by the National Organization on Disability, people with disabilities report a lower level of life satisfaction (34%) than those without (61%).

Even so, laws such as IDEA and the Americans with Disabilities Act (ADA) have opened doors that were closed in the past. We have come a long way from the days when disabled people had to block city buses with their wheelchairs to protest their lack of access.

But we still have a long way to go. Nancy Starnes, of the National Organization on Disability, says, "People know what the law requires, but they don't often implement it."

All too often, costs, convenience and aesthetics are cited as excuses for not making transportation and accommodations more accessible. Yet these excuses would be woefully unacceptable if we were dealing with other segments of the population.

Even as we acknowledge the tremendous impact that laws such as IDEA and ADA have had, we must acknowledge persistent gaps between those who are disabled and the rest of us. Disability rights are civil rights, and they must be guaranteed.

—Julianne Malveaux teaches a class on diversity at Bennett College for Women in Greensboro, N.C.

Heather Morris—No Dumb Blonde

At first a minor character on only some of the episodes, Brittany S. Pierce—played by Heather Morris—has some of the craziest lines on *Glee*. Viewers can't wait to hear what absurd thing will come out of her mouth next. For example, she says to her best friend, Santana, "Did you know dolphins are just gay sharks?" Or she tells Artie in his wheelchair, "For a while, I thought you were a robot." And it doesn't seem too farfetched when she announces, "People thought I went on vacation, but actually I spent the summer lost in the sewers."

Heather says the persona of Brittany just kind of happened. At first, her character was meant to be one of the school's mean girls. But at one point during rehearsals, Heather had an odd expression on her face. That look inspired the director to suggest that Heather's character develop into a dopey and funny girl rather than a mean one. And from there, Brittany was born.

One of a kind: Heather wears a unicorn hat as Brittany in a scene with Chris Colfer as Kurt in season 3 of *Glee*. Brittany's wacky ideas were out in full force during this story line, where she ran for student body president—and won!

Heather worked hard at shaping Brittany, putting her heart into the character. To her delight, she became a series regular in season 2. People who've worked with Heather praise her discipline and her work ethic. In fact, it was that dedication that led Heather to the set of *Glee*.

Care to Dance?

Heather Elizabeth Morris was born on February 1, 1987, in Thousand Oaks, California. She was raised in Scottsdale, Arizona. Her two older sisters, April and Crystal, took dance classes. One-year-old Heather, barely walking, would mimic the dance moves while her mom waited for the class to finish. Soon her mom enrolled Heather in dance classes too. Throughout her childhood, Heather took all sorts of classes—ballet, hip-hop, jazz, tap, and tumbling. In addition, she attended every competition and convention that she possibly could.

When she was fourteen, tragedy struck the family. Heather's father died of cancer. She says about those years, "I didn't enjoy [high school]. My dad passed away before my freshman year, and it altered how I thought. I was depressed—I didn't hang out with my friends. I worked through it by dancing." At eighteen she got a small tattoo of angel wings on her back as a tribute to her dad. One happy moment of her high school years was being elected homecoming queen during her senior year in 2005.

Dancing baby: Heather started dancing almost as soon as she could walk. She watched her older sisters in dance class and copied their moves.

Heading for Los Angeles

After high school, Heather was accepted at Arizona State University, where she planned to study journalism. After a couple of semesters, she traveled to Los Angeles to audition for season 2 of *So You Think You Can Dance*. While she wasn't chosen for the final cut, she was captivated by the idea of a Los Angeles dance career. She immediately packed her bags and moved to Los Angeles. She joined various dance studios and trained for hours every day. The long hours and hard work were rewarded within two months. At that point, she started getting paid to dance in fashion shows and Los Angeles nightclubs.

Heather's big break came in 2007 when she was chosen to join Beyoncé's world tour the Beyoncé Experience. Although traveling the world on tour sounds glamorous, it was tough work. Between rehearsals and performances, Heather and the other dancers on the tour had to dance twelve hours a day. After the tour, Heather joined Beyoncé for appearances on TV's *Saturday Night Live* and on the American Music Awards to dance to Beyoncé's hit song "Single Ladies (Put a Ring on It)."

In 2008 Heather auditioned for a movie called *Fired Up!* She was brought in as a double for a tumbling part. The choreographer—Zach Woodlee—was so impressed with her skills that he added her to more scenes. He then enlisted her to dance in the TV series *Eli Stone* and *Swingtown* and the movie *Bedtime Stories*. The same year, Woodlee was recruited to help with a new TV show called *Glee*. By then some of the actors had already been cast and were in rehearsal. Zach gave Heather a call.

A for Effort

Woodlee needed Heather's help to teach Chris Colfer (Kurt) and some of the other *Glee* cast the "Single Ladies" dance routine. Heather was happy to help out her old friend. He also gave her some inside scoop. Heather says he told her, "'Since you're acting now, I know Ryan Murphy would love to consider you for a part. Look as cute as you can so he'll love you even more.' So I went in to teach the kids with a full-on outfit. I was scheduled to read with Ryan Murphy twice, but he canceled both times. After that, Zach called me and said they might not hire me anyway because they wanted the third cheerleader to be black, so my hopes were shot. But then my agent called a week later and said, 'You're now cast as Brittany in *Glee*.' So it was nuts."

Zach Woodlee would say it wasn't nuts that Heather was cast. He'd say it was because she's always willing to say "Yes, I can" and because she always gives 110 percent effort. Even though she says she's learning every day on set, she still attends dance and acting classes.

Brittany as Britney: Heather *(center)* performs the Britney Spears song "I'm a Slave 4 U" during the "Britney/Brittany" episode of *Glee* in season 2. Heather wowed critics and fans with her dance moves in the first episode where her character was at the forefront.

Her dancing was showcased in the "Britney/Brittany" episode in season 2. Playing on the fact that the name Brittany S. Pierce was so close to the name Britney Spears, Heather's character hallucinates and re-creates memorable Britney moments while under anesthesia at the dentist's office. Britney Spears is featured in a short cameo appearance in the episode. Producer Ryan Murphy said the episode was written specifically to show off Heather's dancing skills.

HeMo

Known on the set as HeMo, Heather is best friends in real life with her on-screen BFF, Naya Rivera (Santana,) and can't speak highly enough of her cast and crew. In 2011 she roped cast mates Cory Monteith, Harry Shum Jr., Matthew Morrison, and Naya into her screenwriting debut. She wrote a short video called "Nuthin' but a Glee Thang" (a spoof of the classic Dr. Dre song "Nuthin' but a G-Thang"). She followed that with a short film called *The Elevator*, which she directed and cowrote with her friend and real-life roommate Ashley Lendzion.

Heather and Ashley plan to write and direct more short films in between Heather's many activities.

BFF: Costars Naya *(left)* and Heather are best friends on and off the set. Here they attend a party after the 2010 Golden Globes.

Besides kickboxing, crocheting, and promoting the Flirt cosmetic line, Heather found time to play the part of Lily in the 2011 movie *Post*. She is also the voice of the Gossip Girl in *Ice Age: Continental Drift* (2012). Meanwhile, she continues her dedication to developing the ditzy, dim-witted Brittany into one of *Glee*'s most beloved characters. And with her great comic timing and deadpan delivery, it seems to be working.

Naya Rivera—No Substitute for Hard Work

Half Puerto Rican, one-quarter German, and one-quarter African American, beautiful Naya Rivera says she wasn't popular in high school. In fact, she describes herself at seventeen as a mess. "I didn't have that great of a high school experience. I didn't really fit in anywhere. No one really was good to me, and I never really had any friends. I was in my own head, I thought I had everything going on, but everyone thought I was annoying. I mean people talked to me, but I was still really nerdy."

She couldn't bear her naturally curly hairstyle and desperately wanted straight hair like the cheerleaders at her school had. She remembers sitting dateless in a car on Valentine's Day, sobbing to Dashboard Confessional songs. And she was obsessed with reality TV,

fantasizing that she could be the next Paris Hilton. Naya even bought a small dog on a payment plan to be just like the reality star. She felt more alone than ever, at the mercy of "mean girls," for the last years of high school when her best friend changed schools in their sophomore year. During this time, Naya poured her heart out in journals and songwriting and kept busy with classes and work. She draws on this real-life experience for her catty character, Santana Lopez, on *Glee*.

Mean girls: Naya uses her real-life teenage struggles in high school to understand the character of cheerleader Santana Lopez.

May 4, 2007

Fewer call themselves multiracial; Less than 2% checked multiple Census slots

From the Pages of
USA TODAY
The share of Americans who identify themselves as multiracial has shrunk this decade, an unexpected trend in an increasingly diverse nation.

About 1.9% of the people checked off more than one race in a 2005 Census Bureau survey of 3 million households, a meaningful decline from two surveys in 2000.

The data show that the nation continues to wrestle with racial identity even in the face of growing diversity, says Reynolds Farley, a research scientist at the University of Michigan's Institute for Social Research, who analyzed the trend. "We're a society where we still basically assume everyone is in one race," he says.

Multiracial groups fought that concept in the 1990s. The small but vocal movement gained momentum in 1997 after golfer Tiger Woods proclaimed his race "Cablinasian"—for Caucasian, black, American Indian and Asian. The spotlight hit other multiracial celebrities, including singer Mariah Carey, actress Halle Berry and Yankees shortstop Derek Jeter.

Mixed-race Americans lobbied the government to stop requiring people to choose one race category on Census and other federal forms. The 2000 Census for the first time allowed people to check more than one race. About 2.4%, or 6.8 million people, did so in the full Census.

The drop to 1.9% in 2005 is "a slight decrease but statistically significant," Farley says.

Jungmiwha Bullock, president of the Association of MultiEthnic Americans, is not surprised. Some believe that identifying more than one race negates [erases] racial identity, she says. "To say you're black and Asian doesn't mean you're not black," she says. "I don't say I'm half black and half Korean. I'm 100% black, and I'm 100% Korean."

The Census numbers "clearly underestimate how many people are mixed race," says Daniel Lichter, a professor at Cornell University [in New York] who has studied intermarriages. "People aren't willing to define themselves as such."

—Haya El Nasser

Busy Body

Naya Marie Rivera was born on January 12, 1987, in Valencia, California. She was named after a character her mom saw on an episode of TV's *Fantasy Island*. She has a younger brother, Mychal (a football player), and a younger sister, Nickayla (a model).

Naya's mom and dad moved to Los Angeles so her mom could model. The modeling agent signed Naya as well, booking her to be in a commercial for Kmart when she was nine months old. More commercials followed. By four years of age, Naya was in a sitcom called *The Royal Family*. Over the next ten years, initially with her mom as her manager and acting coach, she received small roles in TV shows such as *The Fresh Prince of Bel-Air, Family Matters, Live Shot, Baywatch, Smart Guy, House Blend, Even Stevens, The Master of Disguise, 8 Simple Rules,* and *The Bernie Mac Show*. For both *Family Matters* and *Bernie Mac*, she was hired for a one-time appearance and was then signed for several episodes. Meanwhile, she did vocal training and rehearsals three times a week. She also took voice lessons for five years and participated in talent shows. And she made time to write songs and work in a music studio.

Family matters: Naya *(center)*; her mother, Yolanda Rivera; and brother, Mychal Rivera, celebrate Naya's birthday in Las Vegas, Nevada, in January 2012. Naya also has a younger sister, Nickayla.

No before Yes

Naya knows what it's like to be told no for years at a time. Her audition for *Glee* in 2009 came after a period of not working in the industry. Not that she ever slowed down in between acting gigs. She worked as a greeter at an Abercrombie & Fitch store and then quit that job. Her next job was working in telemarketing for a golf course. There, she sold memberships and took potential members on tours of the site. She'd just been cast in a role without much future—a dead body on *CSI*—when her manager told her about an opportunity to combine her two loves of music and acting.

The opportunity was to audition for a role on *Glee*. She chose the Bee Gees song "Emotion" for her audition and was excited to be hired for the pilot. Even more thrilling was being signed for the first thirteen episodes as the recurring character Santana. She was even more excited to become a series regular in season 2. Audiences responded well to her character, especially when her mean-girl facade was revealed to be coming from a place of pain.

Coming Out

In season 2, a story line focused on Santana's need to be popular and her confusion about being in love with her best friend, Brittany. The show's writers had thought about the idea of Santana being bisexual. Audience demand to see the two cheerleaders

USA TODAY Snapshots®

Violence in public schools

Of the USA's 80,454 public schools, the percentage that reported violent incidents[1], by school level, in 2003-04:

74% Primary
94% Middle
96% High
85% Combined schools

1 – Violent incidents include rape or sexual battery, physical attack or fight with or without a weapon, and robbery with or without a weapon.
Source: U.S. Department of Education School Survey on Crime and Safety, 2004

By Tracey Wong Briggs and Alejandro Gonzalez, USA TODAY, 2007

as a romantic couple led to a plotline in which Santana confronts her lesbianism. Naya says the response has been incredible. She gets hundreds of letters from teenage girls thanking her for her sensitive portrayal of their own lives as young lesbians.

Jarrett Barrios, then president of the Gay & Lesbian Alliance Against Defamation (GLAAD), praised the show. He says that the story line of Santana's struggle with her sexuality was one that hadn't been shown on a prime-time show at that level of popularity, especially for a gay teen of color. Like many people, Barrios believes that respect, tolerance, and acceptance can come simply by telling stories like these.

Naya hosted the GLADD Media Awards in May 2011. The same month, she announced that she had inked a record deal with Columbia Records and would be working on a solo album. Seriously inked herself, Naya sports five tattoos—a large cross on her lower back, a small peace sign on the inside of her left ankle, a small bow on the back of her neck, the word *Love* written in Hebrew on the inside of her right wrist, and a shooting star on the top of her right foot.

Bright Future

This shooting star tweeted, "My goal in life is to be a hybrid of Ryan Murphy and Oprah," a sign that she doesn't expect to slow down anytime soon. Instead, she jokes that she wants to build an empire; have a family; be the next J.Lo (singer-actress Jennifer Lopez); and meanwhile, give back to the community. Naya admits she can be a bit career obsessed. She jokes that her perfect day would be going to work and then getting a call to say she had more work. She says the entertainment industry is her life. Yet she warns others that if this is the life they want, they need to know what they're getting into. "First, sit down and figure out if this is really what you want to do, because it takes 150% commitment. You can't be wishy-washy, it's hard. Be prepared for a million-and-a-half nos. You probably will not get a job for a while. But when you do book that job, it is so much fun. It is the most amazing feeling to be on set and to be doing what you love every single day."

A biting comedy for

Gleeks: Jane Lynch (*left*) and Matthew Morrison show off the *Glee* "L" sign at the premiere of the show in 2009. The two are bitter enemies on-screen but good friends offscreen.

Jane Lynch and Matthew Morrison

A Force of Nature

In an ensemble cast, it's often hard to pinpoint one star. But fans and cast agree. Jane Lynch is a standout. Playing Sue Sylvester, the ruthless cheerleading coach intent on destroying the glee club, Jane may not have the screen time of the other characters. But somehow she always ends up stealing the show. Coach Sylvester's acid tongue and evil schemes provide a comedic balance to the positive, self-empowerment feel of the rest of the show.

Jane was born and raised in Dolton, a small town of twenty-five thousand south of Chicago, Illinois. Her father, Frank, was a banker, and her mom, Eileen, was a homemaker. When Jane was seven, the family discovered she was deaf in her right ear. She says that explains her crooked mouth. She's always shooting the sound out of her mouth toward her good ear. Raised Catholic, Jane says she had a nice upbringing but always felt undervalued. She wanted people to think she was *really* special. She had an active imagination and fantasized that she would one day appear on TV in *The Brady Bunch* or *The Mary Tyler Moore Show*.

Learning Not to Quit

Jane attended Thornridge High School and mingled with all the different groups in her school. When she was fourteen, she was cast in a school play—*The Ugly Duckling*—but ended up quitting out of fear. She then received a reputation as a quitter and was never cast again.

The lesson stayed with her. She says, "That was the last thing I ever quit. That was the last time I ever said no." Despite her early stage fright, Jane went on

Young Jane: By the time Jane was a junior in high school in the 1970s, she was interested in acting.

to study acting at Illinois State University and at graduate school at Cornell University in New York. At Cornell there were only six other students in her class. For that reason, she received a lot of stage time. She recalls it was like boot camp and that she was forced to play characters she never would have otherwise. She played ingénues (young innocent girls) and old women. She learned how to fence, and she had to dance and sing.

After graduate school, Jane auditioned for the Second City comedy group, a theater group in Chicago that was famous for grooming performers for careers at *Saturday Night Live*. While she wasn't accepted for the resident troupe, she joined the touring company. She says it was a blast. She learned improvisation and sketch comedy by having to perform every night for months on end. After three years, she was let go. She began acting in plays at Chicago's prestigious Steppenwolf Theatre.

She also joined friends at the Annoyance Theater in Chicago. There the cast re-created TV episodes live onstage. Jane played the mom—Carol Brady—in *The Real Live Brady Bunch*. Conan O'Brien sidekick Andy Richter played the dad, Mike Brady. Around this time, Jane admitted she was an alcoholic. She joined Alcoholics Anonymous in 1991 and has been sober ever since. She also came out as a lesbian to her family, who were very supportive.

In 1993 she was cast as a forensic scientist in a film *The Fugitive*. Excited for a Hollywood career, she moved to Los Angeles. There she performed comedy sketches at night after her daytime job doing voice-overs for commercials. Occasionally, she played roles in the ads. Her most memorable ad was for a product called Nexium. In this ad, she stood on a cliff declaring, "I am every woman who's ever suffered from acid reflux!" She says that commercial paid for her house!

From Cereal to Serials

She also took a job in an ad for Frosted Flakes cereal. The ad happened to be directed by Christopher Guest. A chance meeting with Guest some months later led to Jane's breakout role as a lesbian dog

Guest star: Jane *(left)* played a dog trainer in a relationship with the dog's owner, played by Jennifer Coolidge *(right)*, in the 2000 movie *Best in Show*. The role introduced Jane to director Christopher Guest, and she appeared in two more of his movies.

handler in his movie *Best in Show*. Her free-form improvising impressed Guest. He cast her in *A Mighty Wind* (2003) and in *For Your Consideration* (2006).

During her time in Los Angeles, Jane appeared in more than sixty movies and seventy television shows, including *Married with Children* and *Arrested Development*. She says, "When I was young and hungry, I looked at every audition as an opportunity for someone to say: 'I discovered her.' I went in with a full characterization, and whether it was a good scene or a bad scene, I made it work. I prided myself on that. People were always grateful, whether I got the job or not."

By 2008 she was receiving a lot of work. She appeared in six feature films and was a regular guest star on three hit television shows that year. The shows included Showtime's *The L Word*, CBS's *Criminal Minds*, and the sitcom *Two and a Half Men*. The highlight was appearing alongside Meryl Streep as the sister of famous chef Julia Child in the movie *Julie and Julia* (2009).

September 12, 2011

Jane Lynch shares
'Happy Accidents' of life

<u>From the Pages of</u>
<u>USA TODAY</u>

Jane Lynch might be considered a bit of a late bloomer. But what a bloom.

In the past two years, the actress, 51, became a big-name star via Fox's *Glee*, won an Emmy, a Golden Globe and a People's Choice Award, married clinical psychologist Lara Embry and began renovations on her house. She hosted the 2011 Emmys. And she squeezed in a memoir, *Happy Accidents*.

The book chronicles her life from growing up in a loving family outside Chicago to her acting experiences, and to her personal relationships. It carries a comic tone but also addresses Lynch's tougher challenges, including her time drinking (she stopped in 1991), and conveys her philosophy of embracing life as it is instead of how we wish it were.

"I wasted a lot of time not liking what is," she says, but she took a constructive approach, too. "I said yes to everything, even though I thought I should be over here or over there, and I ended up getting a better life than I ever imagined for myself. It looks like a series of happy accidents when it was really just me kind of saying yes and being really prepared."

After studying acting at Illinois State and Cornell, Lynch sought roles in New York and Chicago. At one point, she hosted a home-shopping show. She performed with Chicago's famed Second City comedy troupe, though she never became a regular cast member, despite her best efforts. When the Second City door shut, another opened at the acclaimed Steppenwolf Theatre.

"The base of Sue is The Angry Lady," she says of a stage role she created in the '90s of a critical, by-the-books scold based on some of her earlier behavior. "There's such a tenderness being protected by Sue. She's a warrior to protect her own little vulnerability. That's why she goes after other people's vulnerabilities. It's Psychology 101."

Matthew Morrison, who plays her *Glee* nemesis, Will Schuester, points out some ways Lynch differs from Sue.

"She's a grounded, earthy person, very humble and rooted," says Morrison, who calls Lynch his best friend on the show. He appreciates her acting skills. "I feel like she really upped my game as far as comedy. She taught me a lot, just watching her timing. More than anything, it's her body language, her mannerisms."

'Tender stuff' for Sue

Sue may frequently be the bad guy, but she's not without saving grace, Lynch says. "She's not dangerous. She's laughable. We get a great kick out of her, and they give me enough tender stuff to keep people from absolutely despising me."

Lynch may have learned much over the years, but she says she still has plenty to work on. Like what? "That's for the next book."

Frenemies: Jane and Matthew get ready for a scene during the first season of *Glee*. Jane's character Sue Sylvester has been the enemy of the glee club from the very start. Matthew plays Will Schuester, the glee instructor Sue sees as her nemesis.

—Bill Keveney

Archenemy

When *Glee* was developed, the main source of conflict for the glee club was the rival club Vocal Adrenaline. But then a TV executive suggested the writers add new tension through a rival within the school itself. After a moment's thought, Ryan Murphy responded, "I think I know who that's going to be. I think it's a cheerleading coach named Sue Sylvester. And I think we can get Jane Lynch." Jane was available, and coach Sue Sylvester was born.

Jane says she loves playing Sue, particularly because of her many

layers. Yes, she's vindictive and merciless. But at other times, she is tender and caring. The writers carefully balance her heartlessness with sympathetic scenes. Her softer side was mainly shown through the relationship with her sister Sharon, who had Down syndrome and died in season 2. Sue's also kind to the glee club and to its coach, Mr. Schuester—between bouts of trying to destroy them both.

Jane herself is much more easygoing. She's happily married to clinical psychologist Lara Embry. The couple lives together with Lara's daughter Haden. Jane

Tough talker: Jane plays Cheerios coach Sue Sylvester in a scene with Becky Jackson, played by Lauren Potter. Sue's story line with Becky, a cheerleader with Down syndrome, allows the audience to see Sue's softer side.

says appearing on *Glee* is the icing on the cake. "I think I really needed some professional success. I would have had to find a way to be happy without it, but I think [*Glee*] really did help me get a sense of myself and a confidence. I think if I had just done *Best in Show* and that was it for me, [I] think I would have been able to rest. I really feel like everything after that has been kind of gravy," she says. "What I don't think I would have been happy without is Lara and Haden."

Matthew Morrison— Quiet Achiever

Will Schuester may not be having the best high school experience, but the man who plays him, Matthew Morrison, had the sort of charmed high school years most of us

Family time: Jane *(left)*; her wife, Lara Embry; and Lara's daughter Haden attend a *Glee* sing-along event at a high school in California in 2011.

dream about. He was captain of his school's soccer team, was elected class president and prom king, and dated the homecoming queen.

Matthew (known as Matty Fresh, or Triple Threat on the set) was born on October 30, 1978, on the Fort Ord army base in Northern California. Both his mom, Mary, and dad, Tom, were army nurses. They moved frequently until Matt was about ten. At that point, his dad enrolled at the University of Southern California to become a midwife.

"I grew up as an only child," Matthew says. "My parents weren't great conversationalists. We had a quiet house. I'm not very verbal." That same year, Matthew spent the summer with his grandparents in Arizona. They enrolled him and a cousin in a children's theater camp.

It was onstage singing and dancing in a production called *The Herdmans Go to Camp* that Matthew found his voice and passion.

He continued performing after that summer. He took ballet, jazz, and tap dancing classes and participated in youth theater. Matthew says he was particularly inspired by famous masculine actors—dancers such as Gene Kelly and Patrick Swayze.

In his teens, he attended Orange County High School of the Arts (OCHSA), a school for students with talents in the performing, visual, and literary arts. It was the perfect environment for an aspiring actor.

Dance man: Matthew does some disco dancing during high school in the 1990s. He was involved in many different activities in high school, including mountain climbing and pinball club.

Fresh Step to Broadway... and Beyond

Matthew briefly dreamed of becoming a professional soccer player. But by his sophomore year, he knew he would move to New York. His idols—including movie actors James Dean and Marlon Brando—were East Coast actors. He valued the careers they had developed because they earned respect, not just fame. Matthew was accepted into New York University's prestigious Tisch School of the Arts, where he lasted two years. Matthew says he felt limited by the school's strict no-auditions policy. He also felt he was relearning a lot of what he'd already covered at OCHSA.

So he briefly joined a fake boy band for the *Late Show with David Letterman* called Fresh Step (named after the kitty litter). The choreographer for Fresh Step was also the choreographer for Broadway's *Footloose*. He helped Matthew make his Broadway debut in 1998 as a replacement in the ensemble. To make ends meet, Matthew also worked as a busboy, bartender, singing waiter, and as a clerk at a GAP store. He put his restaurant experience to work with a tiny role as a busboy in TV's *Sex in the City* in 1999. Matthew then appeared as the replacement for Phantom in the 2000 revival of *The Rocky Horror Picture Show*. The following year, Matthew was recruited for a boy band called LMNT. (The band is pronounced like the word *element*, but

Boy band: Matthew *(second from left)* was briefly a member of LMNT in 2001. He wasn't happy in the group and left to pursue acting roles on Broadway.

Matthew pronounces it like the word *lament*, which means "regret.")
The group was made up of young men who didn't make the cut for
MTV's first season of *Making the Band*. Matt describes the experience
as embarrassing and the worst year of his life. He left before the band's
first CD was released, and he went on to audition for Broadway shows.

The result was a starring role as Link Larkin from 2002 to 2004
in the musical adaptation of John Waters's classic film *Hairspray*. The
attention gained from his role as Link led to a few small TV parts in
shows such as *Ghost Whisperer, Numb3rs,* and *CSI: Miami*. He also
played a member of the gay boy band Boyz R Us in a little-seen movie
called *Marci X* and was featured in another boy band for a Dunkin'
Donuts ad. He was glad to return to Broadway as the male lead in *The
Light in the Piazza*. In that play, Matthew played Fabrizio Naccarelli, a
love-struck Italian who falls for an American girl. The role required
him to speak and sing in Italian and was more opera than pop. He was
nominated for a Drama Desk award, an Outer Critics Circle Award, and
a Tony Award for the role.

Matt's next act was a brief stint on the CBS soap opera *As the World
Turns*, followed by small theater and film roles. In 2006 he became
engaged to soap actress Chrishell Stause (Amanda Dillon on *All My
Children*). The couple called it off less than a year later. Meanwhile,
Matthew was traveling to Los Angeles for auditions or to join new
shows that never got picked up. In 2008 he joined the theater cast of
South Pacific, playing Lieutenant Cable at New York's Lincoln Center.
During this run, he auditioned for a role in *Glee*. Of all the pilot scripts
he'd read, he thought this one had the least chance. He remembers
thinking, "Kids dancing and singing on TV? This doesn't have a shot."

Ready or Not . . . Fame!

Matthew auditioned by singing "Somewhere over the Rainbow," ac-
companying himself on the ukulele. Producer Ryan Murphy loved him
immediately or at least he loved his choice of footwear. "What Ryan
says is that when you see me sing and dance you see a man sing and

dance. There's nothing frilly about me. Actually, Ryan also loved my boots. He's such a fashionista, he was like, 'They're perfect.' He says the boots got me the job."

Ryan Murphy recognized not only Matt's singing and dancing ability but his sincerity as an actor. His sensitivity to others allows him to be the perfect straight man to the chaos that happens around him on-screen. And what turmoil there's been for his character, Will Schuester. There was his tumultuous marriage to a lazy, deceitful wife who faked a pregnancy; a growing attraction to the school counselor, Emma; and the highs and lows of dealing with competitive adolescents in their journey to succeed. Not to mention his interactions with Sue Sylvester, the cheerleading coach who is out to destroy both him and the glee club.

High school romance: The relationship between Matthew's Will Schuester and Jayma Mays' Emma *(right)* has entertained *Glee* audiences since the first season. The two actors first worked together on an unaired TV show in 2007.

Ryan emphasizes Matt's importance in grounding the pandemonium. "Matt's the star of the show," he says. "The show rests on his shoulders—everything revolves around him." His fellow actors say his calming influence extends to off-screen as well. Lea Michele says "He's not overbearing or parental, but someone who, when things get a little chaotic, will settle everyone else down with a 'Hey guys, let's get on our game.'"

That focus has allowed Matt to deal with the attention that comes with starring on a successful prime-time show. He points out that more people saw the pilot of *Glee* than saw all his Broadway appearances combined. Comments about his hair alone have resulted in almost

USA TODAY Snapshots®

Qualities that teens say make a great teacher:

Explains things clearly	70%
Funny/ entertaining	47%
Helpful	40%
Patient	32%
Understanding	23%
Passionate about their subject	22%

Source: Aventa Learning survey of 500 students ages 13-17

By Michelle Healy and Paul Trap, USA TODAY, 2010

four thousand online entries. (For the record, he controls his curls with Lubriderm body lotion.) Matt realizes that being recognized everywhere he goes might not be appealing. But being famous grants him certain privileges. It's allowed him to buy a nice home, record his first solo CD, tour, and be extremely picky about the movie roles that come across his desk. He also has enough money to develop a musical about the life of his idol James Dean. He's also in talks about creating a movie about Gene Kelly. Branching out like this suggests a long-term strategy for his career. "I get it that 'hot' fades," he says, "But I intend to be around for a while."

May 8, 2011

Matthew Morrison breaks out of 'Glee' club

<u>From the Pages of</u>
<u>USA TODAY</u>

He had a Tony-nominated Broadway career before he took the role of Spanish teacher, glee-club adviser and McKinley High's reigning adult figure Will Schuester on Fox teen-musical smash *Glee*.

Morrison is a product and advocate of the kind of arts education espoused by *Glee*. As a youngster, a summer of children's theater gave him the acting bug. He got involved in school arts programs in California's Orange County and was inspired by dancers such as Patrick Swayze and Gene Kelly.

After high school, Morrison moved to New York to attend the Tisch School of the Arts. When he first arrived, "I remember we couldn't afford to go to a Broadway show, so we used to sneak into them," he says.

By 19, he was in his first Broadway show, *Footloose*. Other prominent musicals followed, including *Hairspray*, in which he played Link Larkin; *The Light in the Piazza*, for which he received a Tony nomination; and *South Pacific*, which he left to take on *Glee*.

Bart Sher, who directed *Piazza* and *Pacific*, calls Morrison "truly one of the best of a generation" on Broadway. "He plays the romantic lead beautifully. His acting skills are so high, he draws the audience to him; he has a lot of confidence on stage. He's sort of ridiculous. We miss him."

Sher says Morrison has "the most beautiful pure tenor you could ever want to hear," but it's his acting skill that gives depth to his performances.

On *Glee*, Morrison's Schuester is a nice guy who has the best interests of his students at heart. He says he modeled Schuester on a couple of his favorite teachers.

Jane Lynch, who plays Schuester's nemesis, scheming Cheerios coach Sue Sylvester, sees a parallel. "He's good-hearted and extremely compassionate. Any time I get petty or gossipy around him, I always feel bad because he's not that guy," she says. When the show started, "he was kind of to himself. Over the months, we've become very good friends. It took a while for me to get in there, and he's the best guy in the world. He feels his way around first. He's a really substantial person."

Morrison feels he differs [from Schuester] in one big way: "After high school, he never really had the confidence and courage to go after his dream. . . . I knew what I wanted."

—Bill Keveney

SOURCE NOTES

5　*Glee*, DVD, episode no. 1, first broadcast May 19, 2009, by Fox, directed Ryan Murphy and written by Ryan Murphy, Brad Falchuk and Ian Brennan.

10–11　*Glee*, DVD, episode no. 18, first broadcast May 11, 2011, by Fox, directed by Alfonso Gomez-Rejon and written by Ryan Murphy.

12　Ruth McCann, "An Interview with Lea Michele," *Washington Post*, September 6, 2009, http://www.washingtonpost.com/wp-dyn /content/article/2009/09/04/AR2009090401615.html (October 17, 2011).

12　Robert Diamond, "Spring Awakening Fever," *BroadwayWorld*.com, January 23, 2007, http://broadwayworld.com /article/Spring_Awakening_Fever_An_Interview_with_Lea_ Michele_20070123#ixzz1V8dJIUBy (October 17, 2011).

14　Lynn Barker, "Lea Michele: "Gleek" Beauty," *TeenMusic.com*, August 19, 2009, http://www.teenmusic.com/2009/08/19/lea-michele-gleek-beauty (October 17, 2011).

16　*Glee*, DVD, season 1 extras, produced by Kenny Rhodes (Beverly Hills, CA: Twentieth Century Fox Home Entertainment, 2010).

17　Barker, "Lea Michele."

19　Dan Koday, "Up Close and Personal with Lea Michele," *Seventeen. com*, n.d., http://www.seventeen.com/entertainment/bios /lea-michele-wiw17 (October 17, 2011).

22　Donna Freydkin, "Baby-Faced Chris Colfer Jumps into Glee," *USA TODAY*, November 13, 2009, http://www.usatoday.com/life /television/news/2009-11-11-Colfer11_ST_N.htm (August 20, 2011).

22　*68th Annual Golden Globe Awards*, broadcast January 16, 2011, by NBC, produced by Barry Adelman and Orly Adelson (Santa Monica, CA: Dick Clark Productions/ Hollywood Foreign Press Association).

23　Freydkin, "Baby-Faced."

24　*National Enquirer*, "Glee Chris Hero to Sis," June 30, 2010, http:// www.nationalenquirer.com/celebrity/glee-chris-hero-sis (July 20, 2011).

26　Gleeksource.com, "10 Best Quotes from Chris Colfer of Glee," October 16, 2011, http://www.gleeksource.com/Cast-Members/Kurt/ Kurt-s-Blog/October-2011/10-Best-Quotes-from-Chris-Colfer-of-Glee.aspx (March 28, 2012).

27 Maria Elena Fernandez,. "Chris Colfer's Journey from Small Town to 'Glee.'" Los Angeles Times, September 8, 2009. http://latimesblogs .latimes.com/showtracker/2009/09/glee-creator-and-executive-producer-ryan-murphy-discovered-chris-colfer-but-dont-tell-the-young-actor-that-it-makes-him-feel.html (October 18, 2011).

28 Renee Riddle, "Q&A with Chris Colfer," Chris-Colfer.com, n.d., http:// chris-colfer.com/qa_chris (July 20, 2011).

29 Tim Stack, "Glee's Ryan Murphy Defends Teen Sex Episode," *Entertainment Weekly*, November 9, 2011, http://insidetv .ew.com/2011/11/08/glee-ryan-murphy-the-first-time-exclusive/ (January 11, 2012).

30 Ravens04, "Dianna on Her Audition," YouTube.com, January 8, 2010, http://www.youtube.com/watch?v=sNDz1Nyji48 (March 28, 2012).

33 Gerri Miller, "Glee Club Glory," *Jvibe.com*, August 2009, http:// www.jvibe.com/Pop_culture/Glee.php (April 21, 2011).

34 HitFix.com, "HitFix Interviews the Cast of 'Glee,'" HitFix.com, May 19, 2009, http://www.hitfix.com/galleries/hitfix-interviews-the-cast-of-glee#3 (February 3, 2012).

34 Suzanne Zuckerman, "Dreaming Big: Dianna Agron of Glee," *Women's Health Magazine*, January 28, 2010, http://www.womenshealthmag .com/life/dianna-agron (September 14, 2011).

34–35 HitFix.com, "HitFix Interviews the Cast of 'Glee.'"

37 Zuckerman, "Dreaming Big."

38 Shawna Malcom, "Cory Monteith's Turning Point," *Parade Magazine*, June 26, 2011, http://www.parade.com/celebrity/2011/06 /cory-monteith.html (August 8, 2011).

38 Ibid.

39 Fred Topel, "7 Questions with Glee's Cory Monteith," *Zimbio.com*, March 28, 2010, http://www.zimbio.com/Celebrity+Interviews /articles/Il9FlT2EDRQ/7+Questions+Glee+Cory+Monteith (August 8, 2011).

40 Michael D. Reid, "Aglow with Glee—Victoria's Cory Monteith Can't Fight the Feeling," *Victoria Times Colonist*, August 14, 2009, http:// www2.canada.com/victoriatimescolonist/story.html?id=a0c218eb-f691-44da-b899-76799d32586b (August 8, 2011).

42 Malcom, "Cory Monteith."

45 Nancy Dunham, "A Star Is Born," *YRB Magazine*, no. 106 (Winter 2010): 46.

47 Jessica Henderson, "Get Your Gleek On!" *Marie Claire*, May 2011, 144.

48 *MarieClaire*. "Glee Interview: Jenna Ushkowitz and Amber Riley," n.d., http://www.marieclaire.co.uk/celebrity/redcarpet/34358/6 /glee-interview-jenna-ushkovitz-amber-riley.html (November 4, 2011).

52 Dunham, "A Star Is Born."

54 *VMAN*. "How to Audition for Your Dream Role," no. 17 (Spring 2010): 186.

55 Jamie Steinberg, "Mark Salling Good Glee," *StarryMag.com*, n.d., http://starrymag.com/content.asp?ID=4322&CATEGORY= INTERVIEWS (November 4, 2011).

56 Eva Chen, "Mark Salling: Naughty by Nature," *Teen Vogue,* September 2010, http://www.teenvogue.com/industry/2010/08/mark-salling-teen-vogue-september-2010#ixzz1YPxdMIni (September 19, 2011).

56 Erin Hill, "Glee's Mark Salling: 'I'm Reliving High School,'" *Parade.com*, September 1, 2011, http://www.parade.com/celebrity /celebrity-parade/2011/09/mark-salling-glee.html (September 18, 2011).

57 Alloy Media, "Mark Salling," *Alloy.com*, n.d., http://www.alloy .com/5/86/11391/1/ (September 12, 2011).

57 Ibid.

57 *AceShowBiz*, "Mark Salling Talks Debut Album and Announces Music Video Premiere," October 19, 2010, http://www.aceshowbiz.com /news/view/00036151.html (September 19, 2011).

59 Pam Pastor, "From 'Sesame Street' to 'Glee,'" *Philippine Daily Inquirer*, February 13, 2010, http://lifestyle.inquirer.net/super /super/view/20100213-252859/From_%91Sesame_Street%92_ to_%91Glee%92 (November 8, 2011).

61 Kate O'Hare, "A Little More 'Glee,'" *Kate O'Hare's Hot Cuppa TV*, May 21, 2009, http://blog.zap2it.com/kate_ohare/2009/05/a-little-more-glee.html (September 22, 2011).

63 TTC, "Exclusive Interview with Jenna Ushkowitz," *thetwocents.com*, October 29, 2009, http://wp.me/pusZv-1xb (November 11, 2011).

64 Janice Jann, "Fall for Jenna Ushkowitz," *Audrey Magazine*, August 2011, http://audreymagazine.com/jenna-ushkowitz-fall-cover / (September 23, 2011).

66 Katie Rolnick, "Scene Stealer: Harry Shum Jr." *Dance Spirit*, September 1, 2011, http://www.dancespirit.com/2011/09/scene_stealer_harry_shum_jr/ (February 3, 2012).

68 Angela Lee, "Harry Shum Jr. Interview," *Portrait Magazine*, October 2009, http://www.portraitmagazine.net/interviews/harryshumjr.html (September 26, 2011).

68 Viet Hoang, "Harry Shum Jr. Puts the Moves on America," *Yellow Magazine*, November 2010, http://www.yellowmags.com/Yellow_Nov_10.pdf (September 26, 2011).

76 *Glee*, episode no. 14, first broadcast April 13, 2009, by Fox, directed by Ian Brennan and written by Brad Falchuk.

76 *Glee*, episode no. 26, first broadcast October 12, 2010, by Fox, directed by Eric Stoltz and written by Ian Brennan.

76 *Glee*, episode no. 24, first broadcast September 21, 2010, by Fox, directed by Ian Brennan and written by Brad Falchuk.

77 Eva Chen and Laurel Pantin, "*Glee*'s Heather Morris' Must-Have Beauty Products," *Teen Vogue*, January 3, 2011, http://www.teenvogue.com/beauty/blogs/beauty/2011/01/glees-heather-morriss-must-have-beauty-products.html (September 28, 2011).

78–79 Brandon Voss, "Heather Morris: It's Brittany, Gleeks!" *Advocate.com*, April 27, 2010, http://www.advocate.com/Arts_and_Entertainment/Television/Heather_Morris_Its_Brittany,_Gleeks/ (September 28, 2011).

81 Tommy Wesely, "Exclusive Q&A with Glee's Santana aka Naya Rivera," *Teen Vogue*, June 4, 2010, http://www.teenvogue.com/industry/blogs/entertainment/2010/06/exclusive-qa-with-glees-naya-rivera.html#ixzz1ZSpTiEG4 (September 30, 2011).

85 Melissa Lowery, "Exclusive: We Chat with Glee's Naya Rivera," *Nice Girls TV*, March 12, 2009, http://nicegirlstv.com/2009/03/12/exclusive-we-chat-with-glees-naya-rivera/ (September 30, 2011).

87 Bill Keveney, "Jane Lynch Shares 'Happy Accidents' of Life,'" *USA Today*, December 9, 2011, http://www.usatoday.com/life/people/story/2011-09-12/jane-lynch-happy-accidents/50376576/1 (December 23, 2011).

89 Brooke Hauser, "Jane Lynch Goes for the Laughs," *More.com*, n.d., http://www.more.com/news/womens-issues/jane-lynch-goes-laughs (December 23, 2011).

92   Andrew Goldman, "See Jane Run," *Elle*.com, January 24, 2011, http://www.elle.com/Pop-Culture/Celebrity-Spotlight/Jane-Lynch/See-Jane-Run (March 28, 2012).

93   Keveney, "Jane Lynch Shares 'Happy Accidents' of Life.'"

94   Claire Hoffman, "Hot for Teacher: Matthew Morrison," *Details.com*, December 2010, http://www.details.com/celebrities-entertainment /cover-stars/201012/fox-glee-actor-Will-Schuester-teacher-singer-matthew-morrison#ixzz1iVbb4ggK (January 5, 2012).

96–97 Paul Flynn, "Who Are You, Mr. Schue?" *Attitude Magazine*, June 2011, 52.

98   Hoffman, "Hot for Teacher."

98   Christopher Smith, "The Heart of All That Glee," *LATimes.com*, April 11, 2010, http://articles.latimes.com/2010/apr/11/entertainment /la-ca-matthew-morrison11-2010apr11 (January 10, 2012).

98   Ibid.

SELECTED BIBLIOGRAPHY

Berrin, Danielle. "Jane Lynch: 'I'm Just a Goof.'" *Guardian*, January 8, 2010. http://www.guardian.co.uk/tv-and-radio/2010/jan/09/jane-lynch-glee-interview (December 23, 2011).

Black, Rob. "GleeFan Exclusive: Harry Shum Jr. Q&A." *GleeFan.com*, August 3, 2010. http://gleefan.com/gleefan-exclusive-harry-shum-jr-qa /(September 26, 2011).

———. "GleeFan Exclusive Chris Colfer Q&A." *GleeFan.com*, April 2, 2011. http://gleefan.com/gleefan-exlusive-chris-colfer-qa-on-glee-his-plans-for-the-future-and-more/ (October 24, 2011).

Fernandez, Maria Elena. "Chris Colfer's Journey from Small Town to 'Glee.'" *Los Angeles Times*, September 8, 2009. http://latimesblogs.latimes .com/showtracker/2009/09/glee-creator-and-executive-producer-ryan-murphy-discovered-chris-colfer-but-dont-tell-the-young-actor-that-it-makes-him-feel.html (October 18, 2011).

Gandhi, Neha. "Exclusive Interview: *Glee*'s Mark Salling." *Seventeen*. N.d. http://www.seventeen.com/entertainment/features/mark-salling-interview (November 8, 2011).

Gans, Andrew. "Diva Talk—Chatting with Spring Awakenings Lea Michele." *Playbill*, November 24, 2006. http://www.playbill.com/celebritybuzz /article/103763-DIVA-TALK-Chatting-with-Spring-Awakenings-Lea-Michele-Plus-News-of-LuPone-Kritzer-and-Gravitteor (October 18, 2011).

Gatehouse, Jonathon. "In Conversation with Glee's Cory Monteith." *Macleans*, November 15, 2010. http://www2.macleans.ca/2010/11/15 /dont-stop-believing/ (January 11, 2011).

Goldman, Andrew. "See Jane Run." *Elle*, January 24, 2011. http://www.elle .com/Pop-Culture/Celebrity-Spotlight/Jane-Lynch (December 23, 2011).

Gregg, Gabi. "Exclusive Interview with Amber Riley." *Gabifresh.com*, October 28, 2009. http://www.gabifresh.com/2009/10/exclusive-interview-with-amber-riley.html (November 4, 2011).

Hartlaub, Peter. "Dianna Agron of 'Glee' Heads into Alien Territory." *San Francisco Chronicle*, February 13, 2011. http://articles.sfgate.com/2011-02-13/entertainment/28530853_1_dianna-agron-teen-pregnancy-yearbook (October 17, 2011).

Hill, Erin. "Glee's Chris Colfer and Amber Riley: Everyone Needs a Creative Outlet." *Parade*, October 29, 2010. http://www.parade.com/celebrity /celebrity-parade/2010/1029-chris-colfer-amber-riley-glee.html (November 4, 2011).

Ingrassia, Lisa. "Amber Riley: I Love My Body." *People Magazine*, May 17, 2010. http://www.people.com/people/archive/article/0,,20367254,00 .html (September 7, 2011).

Ito, Robert. "Glee Actress Naya Rivera's Santana Comes Out to Applause." *Los Angeles Times*, May 24, 2011. http://articles.latimes.com/2011/may/24 /entertainment/la-et-naya-rivera-20110524 (September 30, 2011).

Itzkoff, Dave. "Those You've Known." *NY Times blogs*, April 12, 2010. http:// artsbeat.blogs.nytimes.com/2010/04/12/those-youve-known-lea-michele-and-jonathan-groff-reunite-on-glee/ (October 18, 2011).

Lee, Angela. "Mark Salling Interview." *Portrait Magazine*, October 2009. http://www.portraitmagazine.net/interviews/marksalling.html (September 16, 2011).

——. "Naya Rivera Interview." *Portrait Magazine*, June 2009. http://www .portraitmagazine.net/interviews/nayarivera.html (September 30, 2011).

Lydon, Kate. "The Road to 'Glee': Heather Morris Makes Her Mark in Hollywood." *Dance Spirit*, June 1, 2010. http://www.dancespirit.com /articles/2583 (September 28, 2011).

MTV. "When I Was 17." Episode 32. *MTV*. 2011. http://www.mtv.com /videos/when-i-was-17-season-2-ep-9-deena-cortese-jenna-ushkowitz-patrick-stump/1658302/playlist.jhtml (September 23, 2011).

Owen, Rob. "Dim-Witted Brittany Is a 'Glee'ful Breakout Comedic Star." *Pittsburgh Post-Gazette*, April 11, 2010. http://www.post-gazette.com /pg/10101/1049121-67.stm (September 27, 2011).

Ramos, Dino-Ray. "Glee's Harry Shum Jr." *8Asians.com*, April 26, 2010. http://www.8asians.com/2010/04/26/an-8asians-interview-with-glees-harry-shum-jr/ (September 26, 2011).

Rolnick, Katie. "Scene Stealer: Harry Shum Jr." *Dance Spirit*, September 1, 2011. http://www.dancespirit.com/articles/3060 (September 26, 2011).

Simpson, Andrea. "What Were You Like in High School?" *Instyle.com*. N.d. http://www.instyle.com/instyle/package/general/photos /0,,20308601_20360446_20769613,00.html (September 23, 2011).

Sternberg, Alix. "Exclusive Interview: Kevin McHale (Artie) from Glee." *TVchick.com*, May 18, 2010. http://thetvchick.com/exclusive-interviews /exclusive-interview-kevin-mchale-artie-from-glee/ (September 29, 2011).

Thomas, Rachel. "An Interview with Mark Salling (Puck, 'Glee')." *About.com*. September 2009. http://tvdramas.about.com/od/glee/a/marksallinginter .htm (September 16, 2011).

The Tonight Show with Jay Leno, season 19, episode 34, first broadcast November 12, 2010, by NBC, directed by Star Price.

Warner, Kara. "'Glee' Is Back: How Did Heather Morris Spend Her Break?" *MTV.com*, April 19, 2011. http://www.mtv.com/news/articles/1662271 /heather-morris-glee.jhtml (September 28, 2011).

Yuan, Jada. "Glee's Lea Michele on the Show, the Cast, and Her Lucky Car Accident." *New York Magazine*, September 8, 2009. http://nymag.com /daily/entertainment/2009/09/glees_lea_michelle.html (January 12, 2012).

Ziegbe, Mawuse. "Naya Rivera Wanted to 'Be Like Paris Hilton,' on 'When I Was 17.'" *MTV.com*, November 24, 2010. http://www.mtv.com/news /articles/1653020/naya-rivera-wanted-be-like-paris-hilton-on-when-i- was-17.jhtml (September 30, 2011).

FURTHER READING AND WEBSITES

Amber Riley
> http://itsreallyriley.tumblr.com/
> This site offers Amber's take on life, love, and music.

Balser, Erin, and Suzanne Gardner. *Don't Stop Believin': The Unofficial Guide to Glee.* Toronto: ECW Press, 2010.

Chris Colfer
> http://chris-colfer.com/
> News about Chris is available at this site.

> http://ask.fm/ChrisColfer
> Chris answers fan questions.

Cooper, Scott. *Speak Up and Get Along!* Minneapolis: Free Spirit Publishing, 2005.

Cory Monteith
> http://ask.fm/CoryMonteith
> Cory answers fan questions on this site.

> http://thebreathofthewind.tumblr.com/
> This is Cory's Tumblr site, with musings on life and music.

Dianna Agron
> http://ask.fm/DiannaAgron
> Dianna answers fan questions on this site.

> http://felldowntherabbithole.tumblr.com/
> Collection of Dianna Agron's thoughts, favorite quotes, photos, and videos.

Friedman, Lise. *Break a Leg!: The Kid's Guide to Acting and Stagecraft.* New York: Workman Publishing Company, 2002.

Harry Shum Jr.
> http://shumbodynamedharry.tumblr.com/
> This site has photos, video clips, and thoughts from Harry Shum Jr.

Kevin McHale
> http://sickofmyownvoice.tumblr.com/
> News, images, and video from Kevin McHale are available at this website.

Krohn, Katherine. *Oprah Winfrey: Global Media Leader*. Minneapolis: Twenty-First Century Books, 2009.

Kuhn, Betsy. *Gay Power! The Stonewall Riots and the Gay Rights Movement, 1969*. Minneapolis: Twenty-First Century Books, 2011.

Lea Michele
http://ask.fm/LeaSarfati
Lea responds to fan's questions.

Naya Rivera
http://ask.fm/NayaMarieRivera
Interactive questions and answers with Naya is available at this site.

The Official Glee Website
http://www.fox.com/glee/
At the Fox network's official site, learn more about *Glee* characters, episodes, and cast and join the fan forums.

Shumacher, Thomas. *How Does the Show Go On: An Introduction to the Theater*. New York: Disney Editions, 2007.

The Unofficial Glee Fan Site
http://www.GleeFan.com
An unofficial fan site for the *Glee* show features interviews with the cast, information on upcoming shows, image galleries, music information, and the Gleekcast podcast.

INDEX

Abrams, Artie, 7, 73, 74
Adler, Max, 26
Agron, Dianna, 30–36; dancing, 32, 33, 34; on *Glee*, 34; *Glee* audition, 30–31; high school, 33–35; Judaism, 33; pre-*Glee* roles, 34, 35; tattoos, 32; writing, 36, 37
Anderson, Blaine, 29

Bat Mitzvah, 33
Berry, Rachel, 10–11, 16–17
body image, 49
boy bands, 71, 72–73, 95–96
Broadway, 11, 12–13, 15, 31, 59–60, 62, 95, 96, 99
bullying, 21, 22, 26, 27

Chang, Mike, 68
Cohen-Chang, Tina, 7, 58, 68, 74
Colfer, Chris, 7, 20–29; on bullying, 22, 26; early performances, 25; on fashion, 22; on *Glee*, 22; *Glee* audition, 26–28; high school, 24, 25–26; recognition, 28–29; similarities between Kurt and, 24; writing, 26, 29
Colfer, Hannah (sister), 24–25
Criss, Darren, 29

Fabray, Quinn, 31, 55
Falchuk, Brad, 62
Fink, Ashley, 55
First Wives Club, 18, 50–51

Gay & Lesbian Alliance Against Defamation (GLADD) Media Awards, 85
Glee, 6–7; filming demands, 8–9, 63; premise, 5, 8; success, 4
Golden Globes, 20, 22, 28, 90
Groff, Jonathan, 15

Hudson, Finn, 41
Hummel, Kurt, 7, 22–23, 24, 28, 29

Jones, Mercedes, 47, 49

Karofsky, Dave, 26

Les Misérables, 12, 16
Lopez, Santana, 81, 84–85
Lynch, Jane, 86–93; alcoholism, 88; childhood, 87; differences between Sue and, 91; films, 88–89; *Happy Accidents* (memoir), 90; high school, 87; on *Glee*, 6; on Morrison, 99; pre-*Glee* roles, 88–89; Second City, 88, 90

Mays, Jayma, 97
McHale, Kevin, 7, 70–74; dancing, 73–74; *Glee* audition, 73; *Lion King*, 71; Not Like Them (NLT), 71, 72–73; pre-*Glee* roles, 72
Michele, Lea, 10–21, 14–16, 60; Broadway, 12–13, 15; films, 19; *Glee* audition, 16–17; high school, 14, 20; on Morrison, 98; similarities between Rachel and, 10–11, 16–17, 20; *Spring Awakening*, 14–15; tattoos, 18

Monteith, Cory, 37–43; acting classes, 39; on Colfer, 24; drug addiction, 38–39; drumming, 40; films, 42; *Glee* audition, 41; hobbies, 43; parents' divorce, 38, 41; pre-*Glee* roles, 40

Morris, Heather, 76–80; creating Brittany, 76–77; dancing, 77, 78–79; father's death, 77; tattoos, 77; writing, 80

Morrison, Matthew, 93–99; boy bands, 95–96; Broadway, 95, 96, 99; *Glee* audition, 96–97; high school, 93, 94; inspirations, 94, 95, 98; on Lynch, 91; similarities and differences between Will and, 99

Murphy, Ryan, 6, 7, 15–16, 21, 24, 26–27, 28, 31, 40, 46, 47, 62, 79, 92, 96–97

Peabody Award, 7, 74

Pierce, Brittany S., 74, 76–77, 79

Pillsbury, Emma, 97

Puckerman, Noah "Puck," 54–55

Ragtime, 12–13

relationships (on-screen), 29, 55, 68, 74, 84–85, 97

Riley, Amber, 44–52; *American Idol* audition, 44–45; body image, 47, 48; on bullying, 48, 50; *Glee* audition, 47; high school, 46–47; national anthem, 48, 51; on role models, 48; tattoos, 51

Rivera, Naya, 81–85; on the entertainment industry, 85; *Glee* audition, 84; high school, 81; pre-*Glee* roles, 83; tattoos, 85

Salling, Mark, 52–57; *Glee* audition, 54; music, 52, 53–54, 56, 57; *Pipe Dreams* (album), 57; pre-*Glee* roles, 53; volunteering, 56

Schuester, Will, 5, 93, 97, 99

sexuality, 26, 27, 84–85

Shum, Harry Jr., 64–69; choreography, 67; dancing, 64, 65–67, 69; languages, 65; *Legion of Extraordinary Dancers*, 67, 69; pre-*Glee* roles, 66–67

Sound of Music, The, 27, 28

Spears, Britney, 79

Spring Awakening, 14–15, 62

St. James, Jesse, 15

students with disabilities, 75

Sylvester, Sue, 5, 6, 86–87, 90–91, 92, 99

Teen Choice Awards, 31, 41, 42, 47

Time's 100 Most Influential People, 18, 20, 29

Tony Awards, 13, 15, 96, 99

Ushkowitz, Jenna, 7, 58–64; Broadway, 59–60, 62; *Glee* audition, 62–63; high school, 60–61; school performances, 60–61; *Spring Awakening*, 62

Woodlee, Zach, 78–79

Zizes, Lauren, 55

PHOTO ACKNOWLEDGMENTS

The images in this book are used with the permission of: AP Photo/Ross D. Franklin, p. 1; © Bruce Glikas/FilmMagic/Getty Images, pp. 3, 17; Matthias Clamer/© Fox Television/Courtesy Everett Collection, p. 4; © Robert Hanashiro/USA TODAY, pp. 5, 6, 7, 20, 24, 27, 49, 69 (top), 75, 82, 90, 91, 99; AP Photo/Chris Pizzello, p. 8; © Christie Goodwin/Getty Images, p. 9; © Kevin Winter/Getty Images, pp. 10, 22, 29, 30, 36; Seth Poppel Yearbook Library, pp. 11, 25, 31, 34, 53, 59, 60, 77, 81, 87, 94; © Richard Corkery/NY Daily News Archive/Getty Images, p. 13; © Janette Pellegrini/WireImage/ Getty Images, p. 15; © Vera Anderson/WireImage/Getty Images, p. 18; Andrew Schwartz/© Warner Bros. Pictures/Courtesy Everett Collection, p. 19; © Robert Deutsch/USA TODAY, p. 21; Kristin Callahan/Everett Collection, pp. 23, 64; Miranda Penn Turin/© Fox Television/Courtesy Everett Collection, p. 35; © Fox Broadcasting/ Photofest, p. 37; © George Pimentel/WireImage/Getty Images, p. 40; Carin Baer/© Fox Television/Courtesy Everett Collection, p. 41; AP Photo/Jennifer Graylock, p. 42; © Jeff Kravitz/FilmMagic/Getty Images, p. 44; Joe Viles/© Fox Television/Courtesy Everett Collection, p. 45; Kathy Hutchins/Hutchins Photo/Newscom, p. 46; AP Photo/Chris Carlson, p. 48; © Lester Cohen/WireImage/Getty Images, p. 50; © Roger L. Wollenberg/ Getty Images, p. 51; Fox-TV/The Kobal Collection/Cuffaro, Chris/Art Resource, NY, p. 54; Chris Haston/© Oxygen/Courtesy Everett Collection, p. 55; © Jesse Grant/WireImage/ Getty Images, p. 56; Frank Micelotta/PictureGroup via AP Images, p. 58; © John Shearer/WireImage/Getty Images, p. 63; Adam Rose/© Fox Television/Courtesy Everett Collection, p. 65; John Sciulli/Berliner Studio/BEImages/Rex USA, p. 67; Ryan Murphy Productions/The Kobal Collection/Art Resource, NY, pp. 68, 73; © John Shearer/ Getty Images, p. 69 (bottom); © Bobby Bank/WireImage/Getty Images, p. 70; © Paul Drinkwater/NBC/NBCU Photo Bank/Getty Images, p. 71; © Bryan Bedder/Getty Images, p. 72; Michael Yarish/© Fox Television/Courtesy Everett Collection, pp. 76, 79, 92; © Todd Williamson/WireImage/Getty Images, p. 80; © Denise Truscello/WireImage/ Getty Images, p. 83; © Brian To/FilmMagic/Getty Images, p. 86; Courtesy Everett Collection, p. 89; © Alberto E. Rodriguez/Getty Images, p. 93; © George De Sota/ Newsmakers/Getty Images, p. 95; Fox-TV/The Kobal Collection/Art Resource, NY, p. 97.

Front cover: © Michael Caulfield/Getty Images.

Back cover: © Todd Williamson/WireImage/Getty Images.

Main body text set in USA TODAY Roman Regular 10.5/15.

ABOUT THE AUTHOR

Felicity Britton is a writer and nonprofit advocate. Originally from Australia, she lives in Minneapolis with her two daughters, Izzy and Luci. She loves parks, travel, movies, and new restaurants.